Sew

the

NEW FLEECE

Sew
the
NEW FLEECE

TECHNIQUES WITH SYNTHETIC FLEECE AND PILE

Rochelle Harper

The Taunton Press

COVER PHOTOS: **Jack Deutsch**

for fellow enthusiasts

Printed in the United States of America
10 9 8 7 6 5 4 3

The Taunton Press, Inc., 63 South Main Street, PO Box 5506,
Newtown, CT 06470-5506
e-mail: tp@taunton.com

Library of Congress Cataloging-in-Publication Data

Harper, Rochelle.
  Sew the new fleece: techniques with synthetic fleece and pile /
Rochelle Harper.
      p.   cm.
  Includes index.
  ISBN 1-56158-172-0
  1. Dressmaking.   2. Sewing.   3. Synthetic fabrics   I. Title.
TT515.H3325   1997   97-15277
646'.1—dc21   CIP

To all generations that teach the value and satisfaction of true craftsmanship, building a family tree of artisans:

Lucille Myrick, my grandmother, who can create diaphanous gowns of wonder

The memory of Ida Lemke, my grandmother, who turned a run-down schoolhouse into an incredible home

The memory of Odessia Myrick Lemke, my mother and a seamstress, knitter, calligrapher, painter—how I wish you could have seen my two most important and joyous creations

Acknowledgments

I'd like to thank the following: Pat Golebieski at Columbia Sportswear for giving me invaluable leads, information, and enthusiasm; Joe Walkuski, director of fabric development at Patagonia, for fabric information; Glenoit Mills and their representatives for an abundance of information and interest; Malden Mills and their representatives for taking the time to organize a factory tour; the members of the Oregon Chapter of the Professional Association of Custom Clothiers for their continuous support; and Jolynn Gower, Jennifer Renjilian, and The Taunton Press for giving me a tremendous opportunity.

On a personal note, growing up in an environment of "can-do" creativity, with parents and grandparents that built, molded, welded, and painted, I learned without knowing it that I could make just about anything I wanted if I gathered the information and could afford the materials. I'm so appreciative of having been in an environment where I learned problem solving and resourcefulness, especially from my dad, who taught me the value of quality workmanship.

I am very thankful for the professional environment at Daisy Kingdom, where Pat Reed gave me a chance by giving me responsibility and then gave me loyal support with many opportunities for growth. Also at DK, I'd like to thank Pebble Hodgson, an exceptional pattern designer, who took time to help and teach me.

The responsibility of a stay-at-home caretaker is massive even without the added work of writing. I have benefitted profoundly from my friends Sarah Howes, Mindy Roddy, Joyce Lovro Gabriel, and especially the Mt. Tabor Moms: Deb Sether, Kelly Epley, Joyce Brown, Wendy Steele, and May Chang, who have given much appreciated artistic, intellectual, spiritual, and emotional support (as well as occasional childcare).

The Harper/Howes and Lemke/Endicott families have also given me continuous support and enthusiasm that is an inheritance of great value.

Madeleine and Karina, my girls, have by their very gentleness of nature given support to the efforts in this book.

Last and always, I am so grateful for Will Harper, my constancy, who has taught me to savor the aesthetic of a small moment: a breath, a taste, an open window. It is enough just to have written it.

Contents

Introduction

Iditarod sled dogs wear booties made from it. Shuttle astronauts wear underwear made from it. Surfers and divers wear wet suits made from it. Babies are bundled in it. Patterned with totem faces, celtic knots, and graphics reminiscent of Klee, it's electric blue, vibrant plum, "celery" and "spinach," friendly, cuddly, and warmly practical. It's the new fleece.

The individuals involved in developing Polarfleece and ultimately Polartec probably had only a small inkling of the range of uses and the ultimate popularity of this revolutionary fabric. Research and development was spurred by the demands of baby boomers discovering the zen of the outdoors and by a community of die-hard outdoor enthusiasts of all ages. This was a market ripe for garments that were warmer, easier to care for, and less allergic than wool

and that would retain their good looks long after the trek through Nepal was over. Who knew that the aesthetics of the resulting fabrics would be so amazing?

Malden Mills, a textile mill in Lawrence, Mass., staked its economic survival on its belief that it could produce a fabric that would serve this incredible market potential. Using its knowledge of fabrics, yarns, and yarn finishes, Malden Mills produced its first such fabric in the 1970s. It was called Polarfleece, a name which is widely used as a generic term for all outdoor polyester fleeces. The fabric was revolutionary. It wicked moisture away from the body, and it was warm and dried quickly. But its long-term drawback was an unattractive pilling on the surface after only a few uses.

As other mill owners recognized the success of Polarfleece, it took only a short time for competition to start building. Fortunately, Malden Mills continued to develop its new fabric into even better forms, ultimately improving its long-term performance. Polartec, which was first produced in the mid-'80s, had a beautiful pile surface that did not pill, although its appearance did change to a more nubby appearance after prolonged use (much like an actual sheep's fleece). It had greater flexibility for range of motion, different weights for a variety of uses, and in general had a much nicer hand.

Patagonia, an apparel manufacturer in Ventura, Calif., was an important company to surf the wave of this new area of high-tech fabrics. Owned by Yvon Chouinard—a serious climber, a craftsman by sensibilities, and an entrepreneur by accident—Patagonia was developing sportswear apparel for a strong contingency of hard-core outdoor sportspeople. This market-specific company field-tested garments made from any new fabric under the most extreme conditions before endorsing the fabric's use by its customers.

At Patagonia's request, Malden Mills developed a double-face fabric that has a nonpill texture similar to a sheared pile. The new fabric, Synchilla, was Patagonia's version of what would eventually be called Polartec. The development of Synchilla set off an avalanche of sales during the '80s, when the company's sales almost doubled from one year to the next over a period of two to three years. (Patagonia retained an exclusive on this product until 1987; since then Malden Mills has marketed it under the name Polartec.)

Fleece-type products still account for the majority of the company's sales and are regularly featured in as many as 12 to 18 different types of construction, including recycled fibers, microfibers, and different staple-length fibers, with as many different end uses. New generations of these fleece fabrics may include different surface interests, new yarns, and different cross sections, including multichambered fibers that insulate more effectively.

The cooperation between Patagonia and Malden Mills to produce Synchilla reaped financial rewards, but, perhaps more important, it was also a stepping-off point for a new category in fabrics. Competition has driven the development of new forms of synthetic fleece and, more recently, pile in hundreds of ways and uses.

The purpose of this book is to introduce you to some of the many forms of fleece and pile that you can buy; to show you how to identify the forms for specific uses; to furnish you with information about patterns that give you the best results and techniques and notions that give a beautiful finish; and to provide examples of creative imagery with fleece that may surprise you.

Give yourself permission to make something unique, be it a cocoon of saffron-colored fleece with orchid binding and stitched spirals in Prussian blue or imperial purple socks that reach thigh high. I know, for some, going wild may mean making a black jacket that has red zippers and binding, and that's okay too. Look at it this way, making handmade gifts during the holidays won't be nearly as difficult as it used to be; the difficult part will be stopping!

FLEECE & PILE

In the early 1980s, while I was working in one of the only fabric stores in the United States that had a selection of outerwear fabrics, a new fabric appeared that we had been seeing in ready-to-wear for several months and whose availability in yard goods we'd been eagerly awaiting. At the time, Polarfleece was only available in limited garment styles, but it expanded the possibilities of layering for comfort (see Determining what garment you need on p. 23). After a nonpill fleece with a velour-type finish called Polarplus was developed, the aesthetic appeal of fleece increased and so did its potential in the marketplace. From only a few garment styles available in sportswear, anoraks, simple jackets, and pull-on pants, the range of uses for fleece has expanded to such an extent that it would be difficult to list them all.

Originally, fleece fabrics were used by sportswear companies to develop more technically efficient sportswear. Technical fabrics and sportswear are meant to meet the needs of specific sports or activities. Design elements and specially developed fabrics (such as waterproof/breathable, wicking, or insulative fabrics) are used to create garments or layering systems that allow flexible movement, protection from existing weather conditions, and durability of design and fabric for environmental conditions. The

Jo's outfit (right) uses layers of fleece in three weights (see p. 37), while Sue's lightweight jacket in Polartec 200 (left) can be layered in many ways, including zipped into her parka (see p. 35).

surface of these fabrics can withstand rugged use.

About the same time as Polarfleece's appearance, technical sportswear companies were also using a thick pile with a flat fabric backing as a thermal layer in jackets and pants. The unattractive backing on the pile made it less appealing after a few wearings, and it was used less and less. While the fleece fabrics continued to take over the sportswear market, pile stagnated in the fake-fur market until the last few years.

One of the individuals at Malden Mills involved with the development of fleece fabrics saw the potential for pile in technical sportswear and took off on his own to try to develop that potential, working with mills that produced pile. Research and development, new technology in machinery, and a spark of enthusiasm for pile has paid off. The newer versions of pile, which have been developed to rival fleece's technical qualities, have a wide variety of styles and uses, drawing rave reviews in the highly critical European market.

Fleece and pile are constructed differently, have their own advantages and disadvantages, and provide different effects in style. Weight, densi-ty, fiber content, textures, and bonded effects produce a multitude of variables.

FLEECE CONSTRUCTION

To help you understand the variations of fleece, let's take a look at how it is made. A basic velour fleece fabric starts out as specially chosen polyester fibers. These fibers are made into yarns that are knitted into a flat fabric that looks like a French terry knit–flat on one side and looped on the other. The fabric is dyed, and special treatments are added during the dyeing process, such as a DWR (durable, water-repellent) finish for outer-layer uses or an anti-microbial finish for next-to-skin uses. The fabric may also be printed. Then it is sent to the "napper" machine, which roughs up the surface one side at a time, pulling fiber out from the surface. The excess fiber is then cut off to the desired height on a shearing machine.

This napping/shearing process is used for single-face fleece (also known as single-sided fleece) or repeated for double-face fleece (also known as double-sided fleece). The "right" side of a double-face fleece, where the selvage edge rolls to the right side, has a slightly thicker nap than the back. After the shearing process, the fabric is sent through a stretch/steam process to return it to its original shape and to set the dyes.

Different characteristics can be added by using different yarns or spandex and by bonding fabrics together. However, napping and shearing seem to be fairly consistent processes in the production of fleece by different manufacturers.

Low-quality fleece

The pilling effects of the early Polarfleece fabrics live on in some of the lesser-quality fabrics available. By looking at the surface of the fabric, you can see that the fibers lie against the surface instead of standing up and away from the core. It looks like a felted surface. As the fabric is worn, the fibers will continue to be rolled up with other fibers and lie on the surface. This is called pilling even though we don't see the little balls typical of pilling. If you comb the fabric (see p. 19), it will look better for a while, but it will need combing a few times during the life of the garment to look nice enough to wear. (For more information on pilling, see the sidebar on the facing page.)

A Note about Pilling

The reasons for pilling have to do with the strength of the fiber and its self-attraction. Strong fibers don't let go of the fabric easily, so anything that gets tangled or rolled up in the attached fiber creates a surface blob. Polyester in its various forms is attracted to itself, which causes any loose fibers to be tangled and rolled up with the fibers that are still intact. This attraction adds to the pilling effect. The newer, more highly evolved fleeces show the effects of self-attraction differently by bunching in clusters of fibers on the surface instead of balling up.

Lesser-quality fleeces appear in apparel in mass-market discount stores for prices that seem less expensive than the cost of the fabric alone. Take heart in knowing that their life expectancy and their performance level are much lower than something made from a good choice in fleece fabric. You as a consumer can determine what types of fabrics are available by refusing to purchase poor-quality fabrics for the same price as first-rate ones.

The same is true in regards to seconds. Seconds are goods that have flaws for a variety of reasons. Fabric stores sometimes purchase seconds at a lesser price (or at a regular price without knowing they are seconds) and sell them as flat folds or at a discounted rate. But it is not uncommon to see seconds selling on a bolt for first-quality prices. Look over the fabric; if it has stickers along the selvage edge, it's likely that there are flaws on that piece.

High-quality fleece

A velour type of finish is what you will see in better fleeces. The fibers stand up from the core even if a special finish like a sherpa texture or an embossed design has been added. If you can't identify the velour texture from the surface, try looking at a cross section. The right side of the fabric will be thicker and more obvious as a velour. Sometimes the back side, though it may be napped, definitely does not have as nice of a finish and is meant to be worn on the inside of a garment.

TYPES OF FLEECES AND THEIR USES

It is important to note that all fleeces are made for garment manufacturers and milled according to their specifications. This produces a wide variety of fabrics with slight differences in weights, treatments, and effects from one to the other.

For matters of identification and because Malden Mills currently has the greatest variety of fleeces, I'll refer to their number-coding system for Polartec products throughout parts of the chapter. The Polartec numbers refer to fabric weight. The 100 series is the lighter-weight group; the 200 series is the mid-weight; and the 300 series is the heavier weight. Letters and/or additional wording may accompany the three digits to differentiate it in a particular way, such as BiPolar, S for stretch, and M for microfiber. Be sure to note, though, that other manufacturers are developing their own products that may have similar characteristics but may have different ways of indicating weights, stretch, etc.

Table of Recommended Uses for Various Weights of Fleece and Pile					
	Lightweight fleece (100-weight Polartec)	Mid-weight fleece (200-weight Polartec) and pile	Spandex (100- and 200-weight Polartec)	Heavyweight fleece (300-weight Polartec) and pile	Thermal Stretch
Underwear	X		X		
T-shirts and tops	X		X		
Wicking liners	X		X		
Tights/leggings			X		
Warm-ups	X	X	X		
Blankets		X		X	
Buntings		X		X	
Dresses/skirts	X		X		
Insulating liners	X	X	X	X	
Insulating vests		X	X	X	
Outer jackets/coats		X		X	
Ski bibs					X
White-water gear					X

Single-face fleece

A single-face fleece fabric has been napped and sheared on only one side. It has a jersey side that can be worn inside or out, and it can be used for a variety of next-to-skin uses because of its wicking ability. For the best wicking performance, the fleece should be worn next to the skin with the flat jersey away from the body.

Some of my favorite fabrics in this category are the lightweight fleeces (Polartec100S) with spandex, which cross over well to areas of fashion other than outerwear. The flat side of the fabric is made of nylon to achieve a firm, non-pill snag resistance. I made a pair of stirrup pants and a pair of riding tights using this fabric with the flat side of the fabric worn to the outside. It's hard to imagine a more comfortable pair of pants for fall through spring. Because of their next-to-skin wicking layer, they are suitable for a variety of different activities like skiing or cycling or holiday shopping on a cold day in the city. You can also use this fabric to make a warm dress (see the photo on the facing page).

Some single-face fleeces, such as the Polartec100 in the new BiPolar system (a series of fabrics intended to be worn as a layering system), have more technical aspects. The manufacturer claims that the napped inner surface wicks body moisture to an outer surface or pique knit that spreads moisture rapidly for quicker evaporation. It's much lighter than most fleeces and looks more like fabric for a golf shirt.

This cozy stretch fleece dress transitions well from outside to inside without being too hot. The fleece face worn next to the skin helps maintain an appropriate comfort level as the climate changes.

Fleece & Pile

Laminated and windblocking fleeces are made using one or two single-face fleeces.

Some pile fabrics are similar in appearance to a single-face fleece, but as you become familiar with pile you'll find many specific characteristics that are different.

Double-face fleece

The most popular of the polyfleeces is, by far, the double-face velour, which has been napped and sheared on both sides. It can be used in many types of garments, and the comfort of the fleece both inside and out gives it special appeal. The flexibility of the knit structure only increases its appeal. The majority of 200 and 300 series Polartec is double-face fleece.

Spandex is used in single- and double-face fleece. The cycling tights shown in the photo at right are made with a double-face spandex fleece, which has good insulative value but may be low on wind resistance. These tights are an excellent layering piece with a wind/rain shell garment.

Laminated/bonded fabrics

To achieve a more waterproof fabric, a single layer of fleece may be bonded to some other type of fabric or material. For example, a thick rubberlike

These spandex tights are very comfortable in a variety of conditions, even in the cool and wet of the Pacific Northwest coastline in February.

material can be bonded to the layer of fleece to produce a fabric that can be seam-sealed to produce drysuits. Two single-face fabrics can be joined with a waterproof, breathable laminate for a fabric that is soft on both sides.

However, a fleece surface can't be seam-sealed with the current methods available, so the garments manufactured from these bonded fabrics can't be labeled waterproof.

Thermal Stretch fleece is a single-face stretch fleece bonded to a tricot/Lycra on the flat side. This bonded stretch fabric is used in skiing, cycling, and diving equipment. The stretch on these fabrics is very stiff, so you should size your garment patterns to fit the body with some ease (see Determining Ease on Looser-Fitting Garments on p. 112).

Another example of a bonded fleece is the black contrast fabric shown in the car coat on p. 18. The drape and thickness of the bonded fleece make it ideal for longer coats, but it can be expensive. The additional steps in the manufacturing process to bond the material cause the price of the fabric to nearly double in some cases.

It isn't too difficult to identify a bonded fleece when the color and texture are different on either side, but when both sides are the same color and texture, the more firm hand and the stiffer drape will be the first indicators that the fleece may be bonded. By looking at the cross section of the bonded fabrics and pulling the two layers apart, you can see the laminate attached more securely to the outer layer, which also has a more

water-resistant surface. (You can sprinkle a few drops of water on each side to see which surface has the most water-repellency.)

These newer, more technical and more expensive fabrics are usually harder to find (see Resources on p. 131). Windbloc and 300 Series Bipolar are two lines from Malden Mills that fall into this category.

Woven fleece and stable knits

I've seen only a few examples of a true woven, double-face fleece. The fabric examples came off of a flat-fold table with no information available on where they came from. I didn't realize the fabric was different until its lack of stretch and its ability to fray became apparent.

There is a newer fleece fabric from Malden Mills called Boundary that is more stable than the company's conventional fleece. Manufacturing processes are protected, so information regarding its construction isn't available. It appears to be a double-face pile, possibly a knit with a weft insertion. The fibers are packed into the core of the fabric rather than napped from the preknitted fabric. Its

advantages are its stability for use with more tailored garments, a beautiful drape, and a jacquard type of print in grid patterns.

Because of their stable construction, woven fleece and Boundary are not appropriate for some uses shown in this book, such as fleece cording, fringe, and mock ribbing, and when you use these fabrics, the fitting will need more ease than a knitted structure.

PILE CONSTRUCTION

To help you understand the differences between fleece and pile (which means "hair" in Latin), let's compare the manufacturing processes. As I mentioned, fleece is napped after the fabric has already been knitted. Pile is made using preblended fibers that have been made into carded rovings called slivers. The sliver knitting machines pick up fibers from the carded rovings and insert them into a polyester core as the core is knitted (see the photo on p. 14). The pile fibers are separate from the core so the fabric can be made from a far

The fibers are inserted in the right-hand portion of this black knitted core to make pile.

greater variety of fibers. Fleece is limited to what fibers can be made into yarn.

The technology for this manufacturing process came out of the fake-fur market, which uses microdenier fibers to simulate animal furs. Acrylic, polyester, and polypropylene are some microfibers that are now being used in pile fabrics developed for technical sportswear. As research and development continues in this area, we may see more natural fibers like cotton joining the technical fibers, resulting in an increasingly wide range of fashionable fabric alternatives.

The big disadvantage to pile has been the backing, which seemed stiff and after a short while became pilled and unattractive. With the introduction to the backing of softer fibers blended with polyester and a light napping, these problems have generally been eliminated. Many synthetic microfibers aren't self attracted like the polyfibers, and when they come loose from the backing, they simply slough off instead of becoming entangled, thereby eliminating the pilled surface. The flat pile back has been given a new, softer look with a napped process that pulls fibers to the back side, making some versions of pile reversible. The long coat pictured on the facing page is made from a Glenpile with the pile surface on the inside of the coat.

Pile comes in many weights with different features. Some are light enough to make a sweater dress, cardigan, or sweatshirt, while others are suitable for a winter coat in an even heavier pile than the one shown on the facing page.

Surface designs on pile are especially beautiful because of the use of jacquard machinery. Instead of a printed process, designs are knitted into the fabric with different-colored rovings. This process causes less distortion to the fabric and design, and there is no problem with print registration.

Some pile fabrics are so dense that they need special treatment on the seams to diminish their bulkiness (see Seams on p. 56). The density and potentially higher loft contribute to increased warmth and a more effective natural windblock than most fleece fabrics of the same weight. But as with all of

The brushed backing of the pile fabric gives it a much nicer appearance for use in a single-layer garment, with the pile face toward the body. The binding used as seam and edge finishing is made from microfleece, and the button loops are braided pile strips.

these fabrics, you need to weigh the value of all aspects of a particular fabric; don't choose something just because it's the warmest. Some might prefer to have the compressibility of a fleece rather than the greater density of a pile.

SPECIAL FIBERS AND YARNS

Fleece fabrics are made according to what yarns can produce the nap. Polyester fibers in various forms are the mainstay for napping, but the fabric can be manipulated in many ways by blending other fibers into the yarn.

Pile leans more toward a mix of fibers, with a variety of synthetic fibers blended in different mixes for carded rovings.

Microfibers

Microfibers are one of my favorite fiber variations. These ultrathin fibers can be produced from most any synthetic fiber, and they create fabrics with an incredibly soft hand. In lightweight fleece, often called microfleece, polyester microfibers have a chamoislike hand with an easy drape that I find appealing in dresses, T-shirts, and skirts and perfectly suitable to haute couture. It is easy to assume these fabrics are too

warm for everyday use, but I don't find this true at all. The lighter-weight fleeces are designed to be worn next to the skin, under other layers. They are very comfortable for indoor single-layer uses except in warm spring or summer-type weather. The fabric is comparable to wool jersey, only more comfortable and not as warm. And it won't itch like wool.

In pile, different microfibers are blended to produce different textures, colors, wicking abilities, and heat-retention properties. Micro-acrylic fibers produce many interesting textural surfaces, including a sheared-only surface with a velvety finish that is incredibly soft and warm. It also doesn't have the pilling or clumping tendencies of polyester.

Recycled fibers

One fiber used in fleece and pile that has caused a lot of excitement since its introduction is the recycled fiber Fortrel Ecospun from Wellman, Inc. Fortrel Ecospun is a fiber made from used plastic pop bottles. The bottles are cleaned, chopped into flakes, and melted into a form that can be extruded into a staple fiber. The process was used in carpeting before fleece manufacturers tried it in their

products. (Dyersburg was the first manufacturer to develop these fibers into fleece.)

Consumers' enthusiastic reception to a recycled product has created a great demand for products made from recycled fibers. This has resulted in a shortage of raw materials and increased prices even though there are still millions of pop bottles ending up in landfills every day!

I don't know an easy way to differentiate between a fleece or pile made from a recycled yarn/fiber and one made with a new yarn/fiber. I used to think I could tell by rubbing the fabric between my fingers, but with new fiber and yarn textures, there seems to be little or no difference.

ESP

Another yarn form that has some useful applications for fleece is Extra Stretch Performance (ESP). This is a fluffed yarn that results in a naturally stretchy fabric, much the same as a woolly nylon thread. It doesn't have the firm stretch or the return of a fabric with spandex, but it has an easy give that can be useful in some applications where spandex stretch isn't needed. Leggings, close-fitting vests, or a cycling jacket would be appropriate uses for fleece made from ESP yarns.

Berber

The Berber fiber effect was created from a pile blend that mixed a dark, coarse fiber simulating a guard hair (as seen in an animal fur) into softer, lighter fibers. This effect is currently seen in many fleece and pile blends.

Other fibers

Other fibers that you may see used for their maximum wicking abilities might be Coolmax, Thermax, polypropylene, or blends of these. These fibers have been developed to transport moisture quickly. Thermax is good for keeping warm and dry in cold weather, while Coolmax keeps you cool and dry during warm weather. Polypropylene functions similarly in various weights. Other names can be found for these types of fibers. Generally, these fibers are found in single-face fleece with the fleece side worn against the skin.

New fibers with more and more technical abilities are being developed all the time. So much is possible that you need to keep aware of what is going on in the ready-to-wear market to know what you may expect in yard goods six months to a year later. Check hang tags on ready-to-wear

garments, which often have a particular fabric's technical information right there with illustrations of how it is supposed to work. The information gathered there will help you when selecting this type of fabric, which rarely has technical information available on the bolt.

There is also the possibility of seeing natural fibers used in fleece and pile to a larger degree. The technology has been driven by the outerwear market where a fabric's technical aspects were the most important. Because the mainstream consumer has responded to the aesthetic qualities of fleece and pile, the fashion industry may bring natural fibers to bear on this fabric form. The fiber blending, machinery, and other factors have to be researched, as well as the demand from designers.

We are already seeing the use of natural fibers, particularly cotton, in sculptured fleece. The techniques in this book are generally able to cross over to that type of fleece, as well as to traditional sweatshirt fleece, jerseys, and double-knit constructions.

TEXTURE IN FLEECE AND PILE

The form (fleece or pile) and the fiber give this group of fabrics a vast variety of possibilities in textures. The following are currently available, but you can expect to see many more options soon.

Needle-out

Needle-out is a variation in knitting that can create texture on a grid. A narrow groove is left in place where a needle is withdrawn from the knitting process. Designs using needle-out show most prominently in shorter napped fabrics.

Sherpa

Sherpa is a term that has been used in pile fabrics for some time. It indicates a texture that has a surface resembling a sheep's fleece, with groups of fibers slightly bunched in a somewhat uniform size. This texture is used in both fleece and pile. It has a slightly different look in pile than in fleece, and the differences will vary according to the weight of the fabric and the height of the pile. Sherpa pile usually has better

Fiber and surface differences give fleece and pile a wide variety of possibilities. The car coat shown here has panels of black Windbloc fleece.

drape and more variation in the thickness of the nap than sherpa fleece. (See the photo of Maddy's vest on p. 32.)

Looped surface

A looped surface also has a lot of possibilities. The face of the fabric has yarns or fibers that are continuous rather than sheared off. Short loops come from the core of the fabric like a terry cloth. This is an especially interesting effect with multicolored loops. The car coat at left is made from a looped-surface fabric called "Nubby" that is 95% polyester and 5% rayon (produced by Menra Mills). Though lightweight, this fabric was easily stabilized with a light fusible interfacing (see Stabilizers on p. 41) to make it suitable for this type of garment.

High/low fibers

Pile has the advantage over fleece when it comes to high/low fibers. These are special fibers that respond to heat. Fabric is knitted with these fibers in certain colors and/or patterns. As heat is applied to the finished yardage, the special fibers react by shrinking. In jacquard patterns where a detailed design can be knitted in place, the high/low fibers can accentuate that detail.

Embossing

Another textural effect is a method of imprinting with heat, called embossing. Some companies have used this in a continuous print on yardage. Companies that do leather embossing may be able to do it on fabric as well.

Embroidery

The contrast of textures is especially appealing when embroidery is applied to fleece using a computerized home machine. You should use your machine's manual to determine the best process and type of thread for embroidering on fleece. If you don't have a machine with embroidery capabilities, there are many small contractors that do custom embroidery work.

Surface embellishments

Design details that appear throughout this book will give you special textural effects that you won't likely see in manufactured garments. Free-motion stitching and embroidered effects, appliqué techniques, hot-cut nylon, and stitched fleece cording (see p. 125) can create linear design with color, as well as with surface dimension. Look for other design elements in borders (p. 62) and fringed effects (p. 64).

TAKING CARE OF FLEECE AND PILE

Ease of care is one of fleece fabric's best features. It is so nice to be able to throw a jacket into the washer and dryer and not worry about it shrinking, having colors run, or falling to pieces. That is not to say that labeled wash instructions should be ignored. Follow wash instructions if they are listed on the bolt; special treatments or effects may require special care. Dry cleaning is not recommended for most fleeces.

For the best results when washing, the soap should be dissolved in the water before you add the garment to the wash cycle. This will keep the soap flakes from staying on the surface of the fleece.

The tumbling action of the machine may contribute to the clumping or pilling of polyester, so I turn the garments inside-out to minimize that problem. If you have concerns about this issue, you may also want to hang the garment to dry to avoid additional agitation in the dryer.

Because pile can have more combinations of fibers than fleece, there is more chance that it may require special care. However, if the pile is designed for technical outerwear use, it is likely that it can be washed and dried. Test a sample in the wash-and-dry process to see what happens. Pile will lose a few fibers at the cut edge during the first few washings, but it shouldn't lose more after that.

Revitalizing fleece

Usually the style of the garment or your personal style changes before a fleece garment is worn out. Try revitalizing the garment by trimming off or covering outdated colors and design. I found a whole new life in a gray pullover trimmed in hot pink by cutting off the trim, adding borders, a zipper, and new binding.

To give the fleece a new look, use a fabric comb or wire pet brush to brush up the nap and get rid of clumping and pilling. It is amazing how much you can improve the appearance of the fleece with these simple tools.

CHOOSING PATTERNS & NOTIONS

Selecting patterns and notions can be a daunting task, especially if you are looking for something in particular. You don't want to spend time and money making a garment that stays in the closet because it's too warm or cold, the pockets don't hang right, it's hard to get on or off, or it makes you look like a fuzzy honeydew.

An important part of the pattern-selection process is determining what you need—jacket, vest, parka, etc.—and what you want it to do—insulate, protect you from rain, block the wind, etc. If you keep the answers to these two questions at the forefront as you look at the multitude of patterns available, you will quickly narrow the selection.

CREATING A WARDROBE

Here are some suggestions to help you organize your approach to create an outerwear wardrobe that will meet your best expectations. By looking at your wardrobe in terms of layers, you will begin to see where the gaps are and you can then determine better what you need to make. Maybe you need a jacket that works with a warm vest that you have but don't get enough use from. Or maybe your favorite jacket needs an outer layer for windblock. Layering simplifies and organizes, helping you determine what you need.

When you design garments for your body type, you make decisions based on how you

This hat and reversible jacket with zip-off sleeves are made from water-repellent triblend shell fabric with a mid-weight fleece liner.

A layering system doesn't have to be for outdoor sports only. This cherry red raincoat fits comfortably over other layers, including a stylish charcoal heather fleece cardigan and black stretch-fleece dress.

define your body type (full figure, narrow hips, short, full bust, etc.) so you can disguise or enhance certain features. When you design with a garment's function in mind, you need to define its function. You need to ask: How will it be used? Fabrics differ in their performance under a variety of weather conditions, and design elements can enhance or detract from the efficiency of the finished garment. When you've defined the garment's function, fabric selection and design features are easier to determine.

Determining what garment you need

A layering system can be used to create an efficient, multiweather group of garments. The idea is to group coordinating pieces so that they may be worn together or separately. The layers can be shed or put on to accommodate changes in temperature and weather conditions. If you look at the garments that you already have as individual parts of a layering system, the missing pieces will be more obvious.

Fleece garments can provide different functions in different layers. Inner layers like long underwear, turtlenecks, tights, and jacket liners wick moisture. Middle layers act as insulators and come as vests, light jackets, warm-ups, and zip-out liners. Outer layers provide wind and rain protection, using fleece with vapor or wind barriers. You'll see fleece jackets, ski bibs, and tights as outer layers. Sometimes a piece like tights can be used in more than one way, functioning as an insulator in some cases and an outer layer in others. (Use the table on p. 10 to determine appropriate uses for different weights and features of fleece.)

Layering is not just for the sportsperson that skis, bikes, and climbs the Himalayas. It's also for the business person who commutes by bus or train, the traveller who's not sure of weather conditions, and even the person who prefers a more elegant designer style for outerwear. For example, a basic black fitted dress from 100-weight single-face spandex fleece can be paired with a cardigan made from a designer pattern in charcoal gray mid-weight fleece. These two pieces can be topped with a voluminous designer coat made from a water-repellent microfiber taffeta (see the photo on the facing page). This is an example of layering that will provide several combinations for different weather conditions. The dress alone can be worn indoors for fall and winter. The cardigan and dress together work well in cool and dry weather. All three pieces are perfect for cold and wet weather. The coat alone or the coat and dress fit temperate to cool and wet weather. All these combinations with only three pieces! As you add more pieces, the variations begin multiplying exponentially.

Building a wardrobe of any kind involves evaluating what you already have. An efficient outerwear wardrobe is no exception. To determine what you have, pull garments from your closet that may be useful in your layering system. Lay them on the bed by layer (inner, middle, and outer), including thermal underwear, T-shirts, sweaters, and running tights, as well as the more obvious outerwear like coats, vests, parkas, and rain shells. You should look at garment profiles (bulk, armscye depth, collar shapes, etc.) that can be layered over or under other pieces, as well as how colors will work together. This process will simplify determining your garment needs in a very visual way.

Defining a garment's function

Once you've determined what you need, decide what the garment should do. This is very closely related to what you need, but what I want you to think about is the function of the garment in relationship to the design and the fabrics used.

For example, if you live in a climate with frigid winters, you look for warmth and wind protection. You can increase the effectiveness of the garment by adding design elements like a high collar that protects the face, a hood, zipper flaps, and adjustable hook-and-loop cuffs. Fleece in heavier weights can be used liberally in an outerwear wardrobe that needs to be insulated. A heavyweight fleece anorak would not be out of line for increasing warmth under an insulated parka. A parka liner or vest made from mid-weight to heavyweight fleece along with a turtleneck or long underwear made from a lightweight fleece would provide a lot of insulative value in a frigid climate. To these fabrics add an outer layer from a waterproof/breathable shell fabric to maintain the greatest efficiency in moisture protection both inside (by allowing body vapor to evaporate) and out (by preventing rain and snow from penetrating).

If you live in the sunny Northwest, where it doesn't usually get that cold but the temperature can change as much as 25°F overnight and

the possibility of rain is always there, you want range of flexibility in what your garments do for you. You could make various components from lightweight, mid-weight, and heavyweight fleece. The components could be used alone or in conjunction with a light water-repellent outer layer for our "liquid sunshine" and/or a heavier waterproof/breathable rain shell for torrential downpours. Or try fleece with a vapor barrier for several types of precipitation. (As the saying goes, "If you don't like the weather in Portland, just wait five minutes.") Design elements for these conditions might include a zip-out liner, a snap-on or zip-on hood, zipper flaps, a lightweight shell that folds into a pocket and zips shut, and a billed hat from water-repellent fabric with a fleece liner (see the photo on p. 21).

PATTERN CONSIDERATIONS

In a perfect sewing world (and with computers that may not be too far off), you could select a pattern that would be adjusted for fit and for the type of fabric you'd chosen, with design elements that could be added or deleted at the touch of a button. But until then, we have a lot of

responsibility in the final outcome of the garment. The process of selecting a pattern can be made easier with a little information. Some patterns are more compatible with fleece than others, and nap and printed designs on fleece may need some special pattern considerations. Customizing to suit your own style and taste will make the best use of any pattern.

Compatible patterns

Pattern companies have noticed the popularity of fleece and have added many patterns to their collections specifically designed for it. The finishing techniques shown in these patterns still leave something to be desired, so refer to Chapter 4 for ways to improve on the look of these patterns.

When you look through the pattern catalog, keep your eyes open for the words "For Moderate Stretch Knits." These patterns have the type of built-in ease that fleece fabrics need. Fleeces that have a woven construction or a bonded layer that impairs the fabric's ability to stretch may not work with the moderate-stretch patterns, so you should use patterns designed for non-stretch material.

In general, purchase the pattern that is closest to the chest or bust size of the per-

Pattern companies offer a variety of styles suitable for fleece and pile.

son who'll wear the garment and make adjustments as necessary (see Useful measurements on p. 44 for additional information on fit). You may have noticed that some pattern companies often add more ease than is necessary to outerwear jackets and vests. The extra bulk of fleece may help compensate for the too-loose fit that some of these patterns produce, but the best results come from measuring first. As with any project using a commercial pattern, it is best to double-check the sizing and lengths of the pattern by flat-pattern measuring before you do any cutting. Each pattern company uses ease differently, so you can save yourself a lot of time and fabric by measuring first. (For more on ease see Determining

Ease on Looser-Fitting Garments on p. 112.)

Patterns that are designed for spandex fabrics should work fine for fleeces containing spandex; however, you may want to cut them slightly larger to compensate for the bulk of the fleece. If the pattern calls for a certain amount of stretch in a specific direction, there will often be a stretch guide on the pattern envelope for testing the stretch of your fabric, or the guide will list what percentage stretch is required. Be sure that your spandex fleece meets that requirement; otherwise you will need to make compensations for the lack of stretch. A full bodysuit from a stretch fleece with a bonded exterior fabric doesn't have enough stretch in the vertical

to be used the same way another spandex fabric could be, so extra length needs to be added. You may also need to add extra width because the cross stretch is not as efficient when bonded.

In-store drafted patterns for fleece garments and accessories are sometimes available in shops that specialize in outerwear and fleece fabrics. Many of these patterns were developed because of repeated requests by customers for a particular item. Drafted patterns for fleece socks, jester hats, and mittens were available long before printed patterns for them were. The drafted patterns may not have the quality of printing and presentation that you are used to from major pattern companies, but they are often adequate to get the results you want. Though sometimes "rough," these patterns may be just the gem you're looking for!

Many stores and mail-order businesses carry patterns from small companies that might include slippers, socks, headbands, hats, mittens, and even gloves (see Resources on p. 131). These pattern options shouldn't be overlooked.

Incompatible patterns and design elements

I have some hesitation in limiting your choices of pattern and design elements because I don't want to limit your creativity or your enthusiasm for an idea that you may be able to develop on your own, so I'll present some pattern elements as "possibly problematic." One of the most important things to keep in mind is that different weights and types of fleece may work for some patterns while other types may not. Just don't try to make the fabric do something that it can't, like trying to stabilize fleece for a tailored garment.

Tailored garments require much more structure than most fleece can provide. The knit structure of the fleece would need stabilizing beyond what is practical with most interfacings, and pressing the garment into shape would be difficult to accomplish, espe-cially to get a nice roll on a lapel or turning a notched collar. However, you can still accomplish a somewhat tailored look with fleece by using some of the techniques in Chapter 4, such as using woven fabrics as facings, bindings, and other details; using the flexibility of the knit instead of trying to disguise it; and using more stable fleeces and piles (woven or bonded types).

Though it may seem obvious, it is still worth mentioning that patterns that show crisp lines with multiple-seamed details in sharply pressed cotton or linen are incompatible with fleece and pile. The synthetic fiber in fleece and pile means you can't use heat and steam for shaping (as you might with wool), and the thickness of fleece and pile means you can't make sharp edges and flat seam intersections with them. You can save yourself aggravation by avoiding patterns that have sharply pressed details or places where multiple seams intersect.

Nap

Patterns list yardage and layout with or without nap, and many suggest that fleece fabrics be treated as a one-way nap. Approaching fleece as a one-way nap is definitely the safe route, and in general I keep all my pattern pieces running the same direction if I have enough fabric, but what appears as a directional nap may disappear after a few washings. With new fabrics being introduced, though, it's important to keep aware that a more obvious directional nap may show up.

Pile seems more likely to have directional nap because of its manufacturing process, but the direction of the nap is often disguised by additional texturizing of the fabric during the finishing process.

It is a matter of personal choice which direction the nap should lie. I prefer the look of the fabric when it is cut with the nap going up the body. The color looks deeper and the velour or pile more velvety. Some people prefer the nap going down the body so that the pile is easily smoothed out and lies down as you wear it.

Directional design

You may need to allow extra yardage for pattern matching if the fabric has a directional design. If the pattern is small and random, matching the pattern is not worth the trouble; but if the pattern is large with stylized motifs or large rows of pattern, then it's worth the extra effort to match obvious points. By looking at the selvage of the fabric, determine the distance between a repeat in the printed design. If your pattern is large and complex, you may wish to buy a few extra repeats of the fabric to match the design at critical points. For many jacket and vest patterns, you can cut front and back pattern pieces from a length of 60-in.-wide fabric. To make matching easy, you can lay the front and back pieces side by side across the width of the fabric, matching pattern and design points at the side seam (see the illustration below).

Fabric with a large repeat normally means you need more yardage for your pattern.

MATCHING PATTERN AND DESIGN POINTS

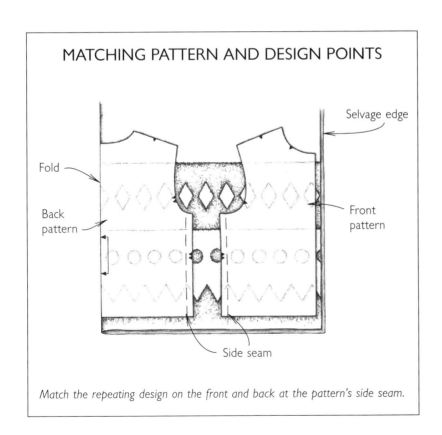

Selvage edge

Fold

Back pattern

Front pattern

Side seam

Match the repeating design on the front and back at the pattern's side seam.

The microfleece warm-ups for Marjin and Kate can be used for a variety of other activities as well.

Customizing patterns

To help demonstrate the process of pattern selection for fleece garments, I want to introduce you to some of my clients, friends, and family. These are individuals that needed either something specific or a group of pieces that would work together as a system, and this is how we chose what to make. We incorporated design elements that would meet the specific needs and desires of the wearer. This approach results in a garment that will get used much more than one that is made according to someone else's expectations. Isn't that why we sew in the first place?!

Marjin and Kate Marjin and Kate are tournament squash players. The courts were often cold when they arrived, so they wanted something to keep them warm. The warm-up clothes that their sponsors provided were thin nylon and fell apart after the first few washings. Because of their equipment, they needed pants with an elastic waist and zippered pockets in a style that would be easy to get on and off over court shoes. The jacket needed to have a full-zip front with flexibility for arm movement, a short collar, and

zippered pockets. Marjin and Kate preferred to have little or no gathering at the waist of the jacket.

They had decided ahead of time that they wanted fleece warm-ups. In looking at the different weights, it seemed the lightweight microfiber fleece had many of the features they were looking for: it was warm but lightweight and breathable enough for aerobic activity without overheating; it was soft; and it was less bulky than other types of fleece.

Several commercial patterns would have been appropriate for both pieces. We chose a jacket pattern that had an interesting inset collar and contrasting yoke and upper sleeves to increase the color-blocking options. The drop sleeve provided the action cut they needed, but they didn't care for the ribbed cuff and waistband because of the tendency of the ribbing to ride up during use and because of the blousiness above the rib. By adding the width of the finished ribbing to the lower edge of the body and sleeve pattern pieces, these edges could be finished with a simple turned edge and straight-stitched with a single or double needle. The pattern pieces were also trimmed and shaped at the side seams and the undersleeve seam so that the

lower edges weren't too loose. (The side-seam shaping can be fine-tuned by fitting the partially complete garment to the person.) The pattern we selected had a higher collar than Marjin and Kate had originally wanted, but because it rolled over to more of a mock-turtle height without getting in the way, they chose to keep the collar design on the pattern (see the photo on the facing page).

The pants pattern was one of many warm-up patterns available. To accommodate their movement and equipment, we decided to narrow the leg slightly and to add side leg zippers (see p. 101) and zippered pockets.

The lighter-weight zippers for the pants pockets and side leg zippers were coil skirt-type zippers. It was difficult to find a lightweight to mid-weight zipper for the center-front separating zipper, so I used a regular sport zipper for that location, as well as for the jacket pocket zippers. The overall effect was just what they wanted. The thread used was a long staple-fiber polyester.

Madeleine Maddie is six years old and going to first grade in the fall. She seems to grow out of her clothes in just one season, so it would be nice to have a special coat/outfit that would last for a few years instead. She also loves skirts and dresses so I added a little flippy skirt to the mix of ideas.

The layers that I developed began with leggings (that would be more like pants for the first year); a six-piece gored skirt finished slightly below the knee (to allow extra length for growth) to be worn over the leggings; a loose vest that can be worn under the jacket; a long jacket with casings at the waist and cuff for elastic (which can be lengthened as she grows); and a hat instead of a hood.

In developing the pieces for Maddie's outfit, I found some great inspiration in the beautifully illustrated children's books of Jan Brett (*Christmas Trolls, The Wild Christmas Reindeer, Town Mouse and Country Mouse*). Her illustrations contain beautifully detailed costumes, some of which depict Scandinavia's indigenous peoples wearing bands of colorful embroidery that brighten the monotony of the white winter landscape.

I started designing the coordinating pieces by selecting a border print with Maddie that she liked and that would work with the ideas I was mulling over. I roughly sketched how the border could be placed on a long, drop-shoulder jacket with a short collar, and then I chose a pattern that had the same general shape. In this case, I found a pattern that would work that didn't have a short collar but did have a nice hood option I may use on another project. It also had a rounded shaping at the hemline at the center front that was easily changed to be straight all the way to a horizontal hemline, which fit my ideas better.

I then added a short vest for extra warmth that can be worn under the jacket or on its own with the leggings and/or skirt. I made the pattern for the vest by drawing the vest shape on the paper pattern of the jacket, taking out some of the extra ease at the side seams (see the illustration below).

DRAFTING A VEST PATTERN FROM A JACKET PATTERN

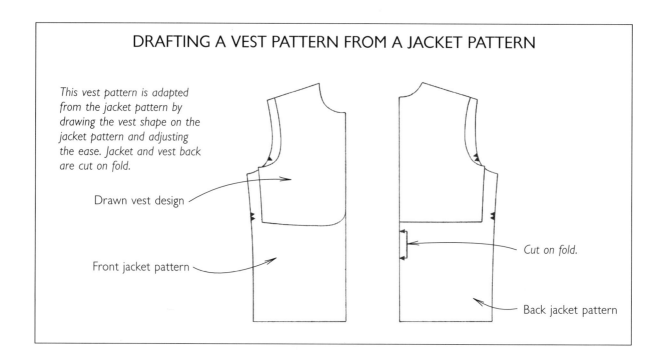

This vest pattern is adapted from the jacket pattern by drawing the vest shape on the jacket pattern and adjusting the ease. Jacket and vest back are cut on fold.

Drawn vest design

Front jacket pattern

Cut on fold.

Back jacket pattern

The skirt pattern could have come from a few available patterns, but I chose to quickly draft a six-gored skirt to which I added a border (see the illustration at right). Drafting the pattern took only a few minutes in comparison to driving to the fabric store, finding the right one in the pattern books, and paying several dollars for it.

Basic patterns for leggings are abundant, so I chose one and then adjusted the taper of the pattern to make sure the leggings didn't fit too tightly at the ankle after the border was added.

The Tripoint hat tops off the ensemble (see the photo on p. 119). I developed this pattern a few years ago based on the longer jester-style hats that Northwest skiers wear, but for a child I wanted something shorter that was shaped around the ears and could be tied on. The result was very Scandinavian looking and launched me into the area of designing outerwear. (You will find this pattern on p. 120.)

A heavyweight fleece with a sherpa texture was used for the base fabric of the jacket to add warmth and some protection against rain. For the skirt, which is mainly a stylistic element with only minor practical value for warmth and wind protection, I chose a 100-weight single-face fleece

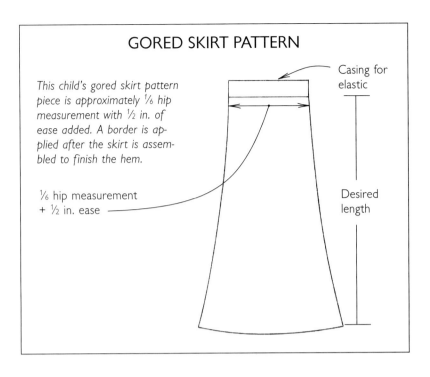

GORED SKIRT PATTERN

This child's gored skirt pattern piece is approximately ⅙ hip measurement with ½ in. of ease added. A border is applied after the skirt is assembled to finish the hem.

⅙ hip measurement + ½ in. ease

Casing for elastic

Desired length

with a slick jersey on one side. I used the jersey for the wrong side of the skirt because the skirt needed to swing freely and the jersey would minimize the effect of it riding up the legs. The leggings, which act as extra leg protection on my skirt-loving daughter when chill winds start blowing, could use one of the lighter-weight fleeces or fleece with spandex, but we settled on the microfiber fleece because of the vibrancy of the color and the flatter texture. The vest and the hat were made with the same fabric as the jacket—a heavyweight fleece with a sherpa texture. All of the pieces utilize sections of the same fleece border fabric.

The notions had to be in keeping with the weight of the fabric and the purpose of the garment and had to be functional when used by a six-year-old. For zippers, I found some odd ones that were excesses from a major manufacturer. The zipper tape was periwinkle, which matched one of the border colors; the zipper teeth were gray, which matched another border color; and the pull was a round black rubber ring that had a lot of flair. The zippers available in this style were all the same length and separating, so they had to be shortened for the pocket zippers and for the vest. (See Shortening a Separating Zipper on p. 96.)

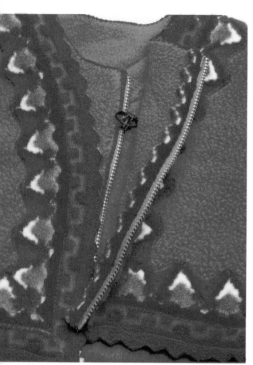

By laying the borders on Maddie's partially sewn vest, many options for border trims became available. Note the border finishing the inside edge of the separating zipper.

Creating a Flat Pattern from Knitting Instructions

Commercial flat patterns don't always have the designs you're looking for. Using knitting instructions as inspiration will open up your options in looks for knit fabrics.

Knitted patterns don't allow for seam allowances, so you should add narrow seam allowances to all edges that are joined with seams.

The shoulder line on the pattern example (see the top illustrations at right) has no slope, which makes it easy to knit but means it wouldn't hang properly from the shoulder when made out of fabric. Using a comparably fit flat pattern, it was easy to redraw the slope of the shoulder so that it angles slightly from the neck edge.

Knitting instructions have edges that are usually much straighter than a sewing pattern. In this pattern, the armscye edge and the side-seam edge were one continuous line, but the instructions indicated where the side seam stopped and the armscye began. So I added a curve at the base of the armscye, which added about the same length that was taken from the change in the shoulder slope (see the top illustrations). A new cut edge was drawn at the side, tapering back to the side seam. (The extra ease allows greater arm movement.)

To minimize bulk in the sleeve, I altered it in the same way as the armscye. Using a curve, I redrew the upper cut edge so that the outside edge of the sleeve was lowered the same distance that the base of the armscye was extended.

The back neck is also knitted with straight lines, so a curve may be added to help the collar sit better; otherwise you could end up with a square corner at the side of the neck.

The ribbed areas (which were made using the double-needle technique on p. 78) needed to be larger than the pattern indicated because mock rib doesn't stretch as far as a true rib. You should make the area to be ribbed the same width as the garment width above it. Then the width can be adjusted for fit after the ribbing is stitched.

The ribbed collar in the illustration was made as a separate piece by using the measurements listed in the knitting instructions and the neck circumference of the front and back pieces combined to create the pattern. To make the collar, I cut a piece 25% longer and a few inches wider than the finished measurement of the collar pattern piece. Then I prestitched the ribbing using the technique shown on p. 77 and cut the collar pattern from that piece. The lower edge of the sleeve and the body of the sweater dress were also finished with a mock ribbing to complete the look.

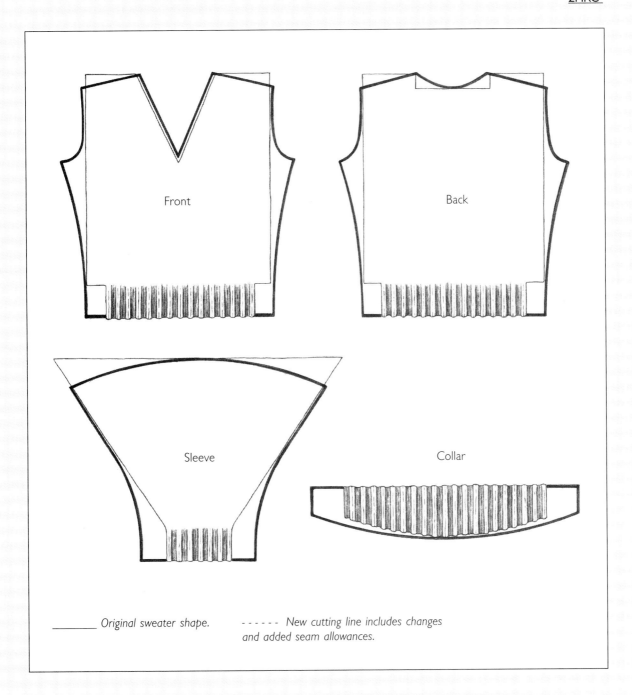

Front

Back

Sleeve

Collar

_____ *Original sweater shape.*   - - - - - - *New cutting line includes changes and added seam allowances.*

The elastic waist in the leggings and the skirt needed to hold up to the yanking and twisting delivered by a six-year-old, and since there were two garments with elastic at the waist, bulk was a factor. With two waistbands overlapping, there are multiple layers of fabric and also a tendency for the inside waistband to show above the outside waistband. To counteract the bulk, I used a strong (but not thick) nonroll elastic in two widths, applying the narrower ¾-in. elastic on the inside leggings waistband and the wider 1¼-in. elastic on the outermost skirt layer to cover and smooth the edges of the underlayer. I really like this particular elastic because when you stretch it, it doesn't get narrower. This allows better accuracy when stitching it in place and prevents the fabric covering the elastic from becoming distorted during the stitching process. This type of elastic isn't commonly available, but it is used a lot by manufacturers. (See Famous Labels in Resources on p. 131.) Long staple-fiber polyester thread was used with all of these garments.

Maddie's ensemble will be used in our Northwest climate, where the fall through spring are generally temperate but damp. Most of the time, the fleece will give adequate protection from the rain, but I anticipate adding a rain shell to this group at some point for the wettest days.

Sue When you teach skiing, you have to be prepared for several different types of conditions. Sue has been an outdoorsperson for most of her life and knows that her very life could depend on the equipment and clothing she chooses to use, so her choices are very particular, and details are important. Anyone who spends a great deal of time in extreme conditions can tell you the possibility of being

caught in a white-out is real. Keeping warm in these conditions goes hand in hand with being dry, and perspiration from the inside can be as detrimental as precipitation from the outside. So in developing a group of garments as a layering system for Sue, technical fabrics layered in a specific order were very important (see the photo on the facing page).

As you've already seen, fleece can be used in a number of ways in a layering system. The combination that we put together may have other layers added or the colors updated at a later time, but for the initial grouping we put the following items together (see the illustrations on p. 36). For the inner layer, we chose a pullover with a zip collar made from lightweight single-face fleece, with the fleece toward the body to wick away moisture. For an inner/outer layer, we wanted a booted ski bib from fleece-backed nylon/Lycra with a windblock and/or vapor barrier. For the middle layer, we chose a fleece vest from Polartec 200. And finally, for a middle/outer layer, we chose a zip-apart parka with a jacket made with Polartec 200 fleece that zipped into a waterproof/breathable shell.

Patterns for this group were gathered from various sources. The pullover was modified from a Stretch & Sew pattern. Modifications to the pullover included lowering the height of the neck and eliminating the ribbing at the cuff and hem. The bibs, which were modified from a downhill-racing-suit pattern from a small mail-order company, had to be adjusted for fit because the Thermal Stretch fabric has less stretch compared to the fabric suggested in the pattern. The vest was copied from a friend's purchased vest (two simple flat pieces easily traced around).

The outer parka shell took a while to design and make because of all the specific design elements that Sue wanted. The body and sleeve were from a Burda jacket pattern that had a drop shoulder with back sleeve vents and a shaped sleeve with the seam at the back. The collar was shaped to curve inward (toward the neck), but I added a drawstring for even more wind protection. Pocket and flap designs were gleaned from catalogs of popular outerwear manufacturers and roughly sketched onto the pattern pieces to see what sizes would balance with the design. Since this part of the parka isn't fleece, I won't go

SUE'S ENSEMBLE

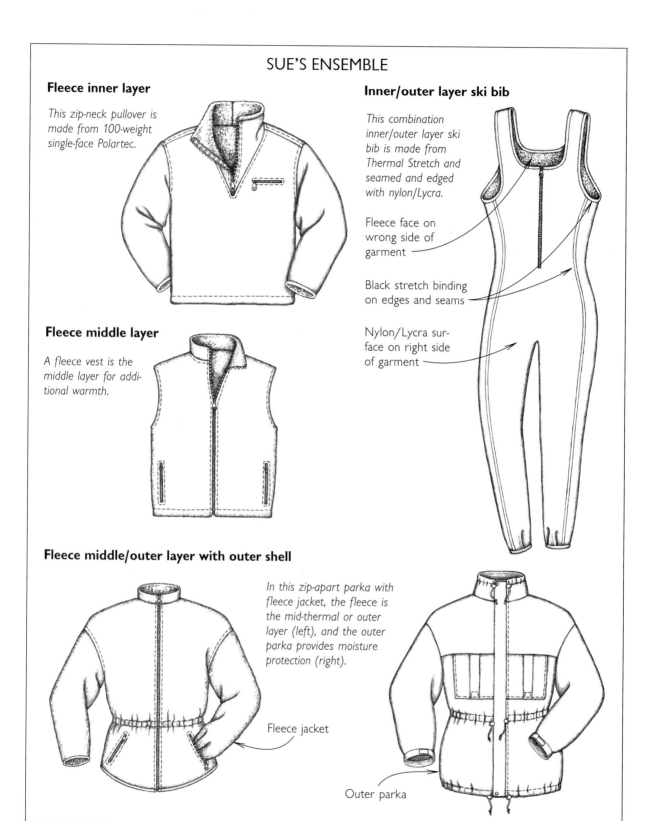

Fleece inner layer

This zip-neck pullover is made from 100-weight single-face Polartec.

Fleece middle layer

A fleece vest is the middle layer for additional warmth.

Inner/outer layer ski bib

This combination inner/outer layer ski bib is made from Thermal Stretch and seamed and edged with nylon/Lycra.

Fleece face on wrong side of garment

Black stretch binding on edges and seams

Nylon/Lycra surface on right side of garment

Fleece middle/outer layer with outer shell

In this zip-apart parka with fleece jacket, the fleece is the mid-thermal or outer layer (left), and the outer parka provides moisture protection (right).

Fleece jacket

Outer parka

into the details of the pocket and flap designs, but you can check Resources (p. 131) for outerwear or commercial patterns that have designs that appeal to you.

The fleece jacket that zips into the outer parka shell was drafted from the parka-shell pattern after eliminating some of the details that would be unnecessary or redundant (vents, large pockets, wind flaps). It was made in the same way as Madeleine's vest, using the same shoulder line and drawing the design on the parka pattern.

By using the same pattern for the two pieces of the zip-together, you will ensure that the shoulder, neck, armscye, and other significant fitting points will match and not cause the inner layer to bunch up. Using the same pattern also allows you to adjust the hemline of the inner layer to be shorter than the outer layer. As it is worn, fleece will hang closer to the body than a stiffer-fabric shell. If the two layers are the same length, the inside layer will show under the hem of the outer shell. You can cut the inside fleece layer a few inches shorter than the outer shell, or you can wait and try on the semi-completed garment before deciding where to hem it.

Other design elements added to the pattern for the fleece layer were a curved hem, a shorter collar that would be less noticeable with the outer shell worn over it, and small hook-and-loop tabs that are attached to loops on the inside of the shell. (More complete information on techniques for the zip-apart parka is found in Making a Zip-Apart Parka on p. 94.)

Companion fabrics for this layering system had to be totally compatible with the conditions that extreme skiers face. We needed a waterproof/breathable fabric for the outer parka shell with all the seams correctly sealed; a special mesh liner that draws moisture away from the body; midweight fleece for the jacket and vest; fleece bonded with nylon/spandex for the ski bib; and a lighter-weight fleece for the pullover. Nylon fabrics were used for all the binding fabrics to repel moisture.

Notions should also be consistent with the end use of the garment. Sport-weight zippers were used in the outer layers because they hold up to the elements and they're easy to use with ski gloves (nylon cording was added to the zipper pulls to make them even easier). Hook-and-loop tape (which is made of a non-absorbent nylon type of product) was used to secure the wind flap. The thread was a long staple-fiber polyester.

Jo An artist with an essential need for self-expression, Jo wanted a layering-system combination that fit her flair, colors, and urban lifestyle. The Japonesque look of the Sewing Workshop patterns fit her to a tee (see Resources on p. 131). We chose to make the next-to-skin layer a top with a folded shawl collar and gusseted cut-on sleeves and a skirt with a yoke and front drape. A simple two-button vest can be worn by itself over the top and skirt or used for extra insulative value in conjunction with the outer jacket.

Jo chose a special patterned 200-weight fleece for the Hong Kong vest. Then we paired it with a lightweight microfiber fleece for the drapey skirt and top, edging both pieces with multiple rows of topstitching for a sharper edge and filling in the skirt yoke with topstitching for a flat and firm high-hip area. The style of the Haiku jacket has a 1940s look to it, and the thick, fluffy fleece we found in a coordinating burgundy solid reflects that era nicely.

To stabilize the long panels and back straps on the vest, I used a water-repellent triblend (poly/nylon/cotton) that has a chintz look to it for the outer layer. The fleece was used as the inside layer at the center front panels to give them the same weight as the rest of the

Jo's Japonesque layering combination has a microfleece inner layer, a mid-weight vest with triblend trim, and a heavyweight fleece outer jacket.

Chapter Two
38

garment. Filling the panels with topstitching made them more firm, so it was easy to apply the bound buttonholes. The back straps were made of two layers of triblend with a nonfusible interfacing and topstitched in the same manner as the panels.

The triblend, a densely woven and very stable fabric, was used to stabilize and finish the edges of the fleece all in one step. Separate pattern pieces were created for the edges and hems of the vest and cut from the triblend, then sewn on like a facing (see p. 61). The lapel of the Haiku jacket was underlined with the triblend to stabilize it for extra stitching and embellishments and to keep it from getting stretched out of shape.

To add a little more interest to the lapel and to emphasize a vertical line on the jacket, a microfleece from a contrasting color was used for a binding, then a black fleece cord was zigzagged over the edge between the cord and the lapel. The same cord edge was used around the bottom edge, patch pockets, and sleeve hems for the edge finish. The thread for all the layers was a long staple-fiber polester.

Sarah Subtle, creative, and elegant, Sarah loves comfort, and fleece is perfect for that.

She likes the cocoon feel of shawls and big wrapped coats—garments that need a body inside and movement to show their true personality. The garment combination she wanted was a sweater-type dress that could be worn with thick cabled tights or stirrup pants and a big, mushy, hooded coat that would turn heads at ski resorts yet still be functional (see the photo on p. 43).

The jacket design she chose has simple lines, a wide, overlapping center front that falls from a roomy hood, full sleeves that turn up at the cuff, and big patch pockets lined with fleece. Initially, Sarah wanted the coat to be made from a single layer of Oatmeal Heather fleece, but after discussing the benefits of a wind barrier, she decided it would be nice to incorporate a water-repellent brushed microfiber as an overlay on the yoke, sleeves, and upper body. The overlay became a palette for additional design elements—free-motion stitching, thick fleece cord, and hot-cut nylon techniques. The design and color of the overlay edge was inspired by the border design on the coordinating fabric for the dress. The thread was a long staple-fiber polyester.

The fleece for the dress is a horizontal print, which many women might dismiss immediately, but the small scale of the print de-emphasizes the widening effect. We had difficulty finding the right kind of pattern for this dress. Sarah wanted a shawl collar and more of a sweater look. The commercial patterns available at the time didn't have the shawl collar in quite the way she wanted.

Then I remembered knitting a cabled sweater that had the same profile she was looking for. Sure enough, I found the instructions. And what's more, there was a diagram on the instruction sheet that showed the finished shape and all the dimensions for each finished piece of the sweater (many knitting instructions include these types of diagrams for clarity). I double-checked the measurements with the knitting instructions by calculating the stitches per inch and the increases and decreases, then plotted them on pattern paper. (See Creating a Flat Pattern from Knitting Instructions on p. 30 for more on adapting to a flat pattern.) We were very happy with the results (see the photo on p. 103), but this isn't a project for someone who is unfamiliar with knitting.

NOTIONS

I've mentioned specific notions throughout the previous pattern descriptions, but here is some important information about notions you'll use when sewing with fleece.

Thread

Weight and fiber content are the key considerations in thread choice. For lightweight to mid-weight fleeces, you should choose a medium-weight, long staple-fiber polyester thread because it doesn't easily absorb moisture, which can cause the thread to rot. If the garment is a next-to-the-body layer and will not be subjected to a lot of moisture, a cotton-wrapped polyester thread may be sufficient for strength. Thicker, heavier fleece and pile can be stitched with heavier polyester or nylon thread, but make sure the machine needle has an eye large enough for the thread.

Machine needles and pins

Universal-tip machine needles are appropriate for fleece, but I've found that needles identified with a "stretch" label are useful for stitching through more than one type of fabric at a time. They are available in many sizes. I prefer to use a size 70/10 needle for a lightweight fleece and a 90/14 needle for heavier fleece and pile.

If you are using a tightly woven synthetic fabric for binding or trim, switch to a Microtex sharp needle for a better stitch. If you still aren't getting a good result, try a needle designed for metallic thread. This type of needle has a larger eye that allows the thread to slide through easily.

Double needles are available as "stretch" types, which are especially useful in a 4.0 mm or wider. Remember to keep the stitch length as long as possible (but not as long as a basting stitch) to prevent rippling seams.

To some degree, pins are a matter of personal taste. I prefer to have pins that slide easily into the fabric but that have a head large enough to find in thick fabrics. Ceramic-head silk pins work well for me, but you may find other options like quilting pins that fit your preferences.

Elastic

Firm, nonroll types of elastic will be most effective on fleece. (See p. 76 for tips on applying elastic.) Sport types of elastic with or without a drawstring are available, but test their effective stretch in a sample first. (For a stretchable drawcord using a narrow elastic, see Drawcord and Casing on p. 91.)

Snaps, buttons, and zippers

The choice of a closure should be in balance with the weight and use of the garment. Smaller-scale snaps, buttons, and zippers may work well for lightweight fleece, especially if it is backed (faced) with a woven fabric. Otherwise, closures that are easily manipulated are good choices. You'll be glad to have them when you have to button a jacket with cold hands. (For more on closures, see pp. 88-91.)

Ribbing

Available in different constructions (1 x 1, 2 x 2), fiber contents, and textures, ribbing is easy to use. You should choose one that has no cotton content and has a good return. One that has spandex or is made of the new ESP or stretch fibers will have a longer stretch life. Also, the ribbing shouldn't be steamed during cleaning because its stretch may be lost. (See pp. 76-78 for additional information.)

Stabilizers

Stabilizing areas of a fleece garment can be a creative part of the design process. Traditional interfacings are generally used in the form of nonfusible interfacings. It's important to keep in mind that if you are using an interfacing, there is an outer layer of fabric and a facing layer of fabric. If both of these layers are fleece, you may have more bulk than you want. But with many garment styles and lightweight to mid-weight fleeces, interfacings may accomplish the stabilizing process just fine. Choose nonfusible interfacings that are comparable in weight to the fleece fabrics you are using.

Interfacings that are fused in place with a hot iron are often incompatible with fleece because the heat necessary to fuse the interfacing in place can destroy the texture of the fleece; however, a more flat, thinner fleece may work fine with a low-heat fusible interfacing. The green nubby fleece coat (see p. 18) is fully interlined with a lightweight fusible (knit) interfacing to add body and some wind resistance to the fabric. The wrong side of this fleece is very flat, and the flatter the fabric surface, the easier to fuse (remember to keep the iron temperature in the appropriate range for the fiber content). If the right side of the fabric has a thick velour or pile, it may be difficult to get enough pressure on the interfacing and backing to get a good bond or to keep the interfacing from rippling.

Experimentation with a few interfacing options will show you what will produce the desired results. I tend toward using flat woven fabrics in a complementary fabric to stabilize edges, as in Jo's Haiku jacket lapel (see p. 36), which was underlined with triblend, or the charcoal cardigan shown on p. 22, which has a woven nylon facing in addition to a fusible knit at the buttonhole area. (See Standard facings and hems on p. 60 and Buttons and buttonholes on p. 89 for more information on woven fabrics as an alternative to interfacing.)

MODIFYING PATTERNS & PREPARING TO SEW

Just about anyone who sews knows that most patterns need to be altered in some way—usually for fit. But a number of people will tell you that they rarely make a garment as it is shown on the pattern for reasons other than fit. Creative people need to make the garment their own even if the change is only in the fabric selection or a minor one in the design.

This chapter offers suggestions—not rules—for preparing the pattern and cutting out the fabric, depending on fitting needs and the characteristics of the fabric. Then Chapter 4 will provide tech-

niques, or "tools," to help you develop design elements that come from your inspiration. Consider them part of a "toolbox" filled with useful things to make your project turn out the way you want it to.

Pattern changes for fleece fabrics are generally related to minimizing bulk, adapting for what is most appropriate to the fabric's characteristics, and adjusting for changes in construction techniques, such as edge finishes or notion applications. To make pattern modification easier, we'll look at body measurements that are useful in comparing with pattern measurements, specif-

ic garment design elements that may need adjustments for using fleece, and how to alter the pattern for fleece with special characteristics and uses. And to help the sewing process go smoothly, we'll look at how to prepare the fabric and cut it out.

Design and construction techniques that vary from the pattern may make a difference in the way you cut out your pattern. Seam-allowance width, edge and hem allowances, and design changes re-

Sarah's shawl-collared hooded coat is made from Polartec 300 with a nylon microfiber overlay (see p. 39).

quiring additional pattern pieces should be considered before cutting out your pattern. Chapter 4 provides pattern-change information for using these techniques.

FITTING THE PATTERN

When you're fitting a pattern for a fleece garment, use the same fitting techniques you would for all your other sewing. The most important fitting you can do is comparing body measurements to the flat-pattern measurements. In other words, the measurement of the pattern pieces at a certain point, less seam allowances, should be compared with body measurements at the same point, with the desired ease amount added. (A tip for determining general ease is found in the sidebar on p. 112.)

You can facilitate this measuring process by having on hand a similar type of garment that either has the fit you are looking for or is an example of what you don't want. Compare the measurements of the garment with the flat-pattern measurements to determine the appropriate adjustment.

Another way to compare fit visually is to hold up the paper pattern to your body or to pin or tape the pattern pieces together along major seams, matching seamlines, and then try it on.

Useful measurements

Some measurements that I find useful for jackets and coats are the shoulder measurement across the back, the sleeve, the back of the neck (at the base of the neck) to the wrist (with bent elbow), the neck, the back of the neck to the waist, and the total length (see the illustration on the facing page).

The shoulder measurement is a beginning reference point for the rest of the coat. If the garment hangs properly from the shoulder, it will feel and look much better. Measuring the shoulder is different in an outerwear jacket because it is usually a drop shoulder, and an exact shoulder measurement is too narrow for a comparison. (A drop shoulder is a way of adding ease for flexibility to a pattern.) Personal taste and body type will determine what is the most attractive and the most comfortable for you as far as how far off the shoulder it should be. Once you determine how far off the shoulder you want it to be, measure to that point (comparing with another garment would be helpful here). Then you can adjust your pattern accordingly.

The drop-shoulder measurement will also assist in determining the sleeve measurement. Subtract half of your drop-shoulder measurement from the back-neck-to-wrist measurement. The result will be the finished sleeve length (without seam allowances). Add 1 in. or 2 in. for blousing ease with any cuff, ribbing, or stretched-on binding. The style of the garment may need more ease in the length of the sleeve if the design is very full and has cuffs.

On patterns with a fitted sleeve, extra ease is added to the cap area to shape the top of the sleeve. Because of its bulk, fleece fabric doesn't look very good in a fitted sleeve cap that hasn't been designed specifically for use with fleece. An adjustment in the sleeve cap of the pattern can eliminate some of the extra ease so that the sleeve cap will look less puffy when made from fleece. A simple way to adjust the pattern is to fold it across the sleeve cap and make a narrow tuck. Fold out only a small amount to start with. If there is still too much fabric, you can adjust it more as you pin it in the garment (see the illustration on p. 46).

The back-neck-to-wrist measurement can be especially helpful when using a pattern with a cut-on sleeve

USEFUL MEASUREMENTS TO DETERMINE FIT OF PATTERN

Measuring the body

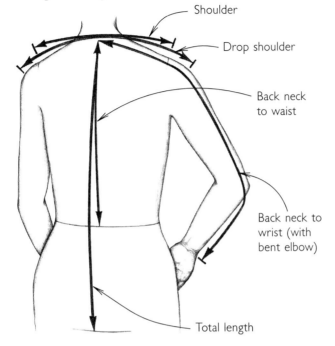

Shoulder

Drop shoulder

Back neck to waist

Back neck to wrist (with bent elbow)

Total length

Measuring the neck

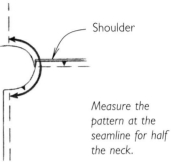

Center back

Shoulder

Measure the pattern at the seamline for half the neck.

Center front

The neck measurement should be compared with the pattern at the neck along the seamline.

Measuring a similar garment

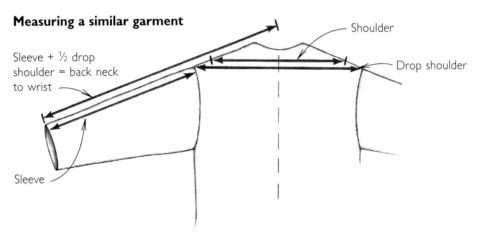

Sleeve + ½ drop shoulder = back neck to wrist

Sleeve

Shoulder

Drop shoulder

By comparing actual body and garment measurements to the flat pattern, you can produce a better-fitting garment on the first try. The back-neck-to-wrist measurement should be equal to the total of the sleeve measurement plus half the drop-shoulder measurement.

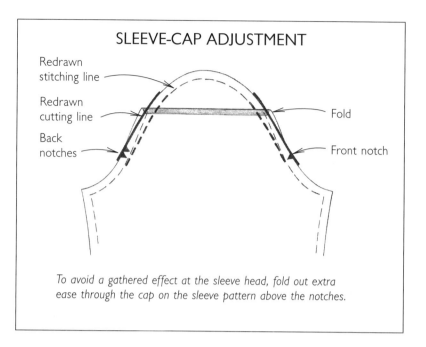

SLEEVE-CAP ADJUSTMENT

Redrawn stitching line

Redrawn cutting line

Back notches

Fold

Front notch

To avoid a gathered effect at the sleeve head, fold out extra ease through the cap on the sleeve pattern above the notches.

where there is no distinguishable shoulder point. With less shaping for arm rotation in the armscye, a cut-on sleeve may require slightly more blousing ease.

The neck measurement is often overlooked for comparison to the actual body measurements, but it is very important. If the base of the neck measures 15 in., the collar of a mid-layer jacket may be 21 in. The ease at the collar is variable because of how the garment will be used. A next-to-skin layer will have less ease because the garment needs to fit closer, and the outer-shell layer will have the most ease so that the collar will fit over all the layers underneath. For outer layers, measure the neck while all

under layers are being worn. This will give you a minimum collar measurement.

The back-neck-to-waist measurement determines the location for waist shaping and drawcord-casing placement. For an outer layer that has some blousing above a waistband or drawcord casing, ease for blousing is required. The amount of ease will vary with the fullness of the design and the height of the person. For an average-height person, 2 in. to 3 in. of extra waist length would be appropriate when a waist drawcord casing is added to a parka.

Total length may seem like an obvious measurement to include, but it is often overlooked. Most important, you

want to make sure the garment is long enough to meet your expectations. A long jacket with a drawcord casing at the bottom will require adding an inch or so for blousing when the casing is drawn up. On a garment with a straight hem and no details at the bottom, adjustments can be made at the last minute. If the pattern has any shaping at the bottom, like a stirrup on pants or an asymmetrical hemline, you will need to be accurate on the length and adjust the pattern before cutting out.

You probably noticed that I didn't mention a chest measurement. If you buy your pattern according to the chest or bust measurement, then the intended ease for the design is built in. The amount of ease at the chest or bust can vary from one pattern to the next, so there is no point in stipulating what the number of inches should be. And you can usually take out some extra fullness at the side seams if necessary in a partially complete garment.

Fitting with spandex

Fitting for unbonded fleeces with spandex requires a different approach than for those without (see the illustration on the facing page). Spandex garments are generally made smaller than the body, which

ADJUSTING FIT FOR FLEECE WITH SPANDEX

Actual hip measurement

Pattern should measure

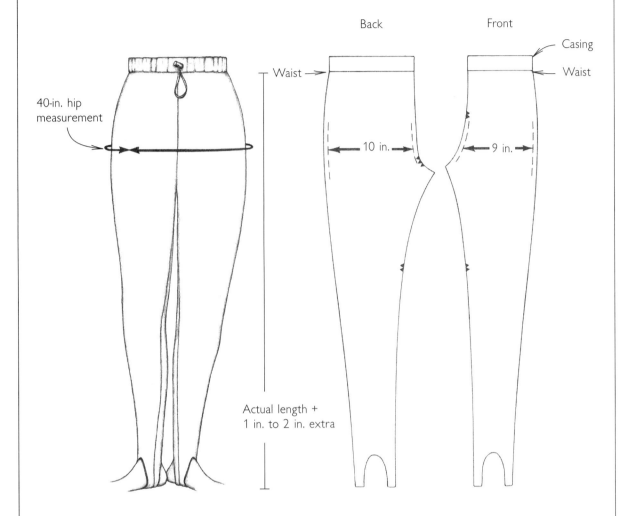

40-in. hip measurement

Back

Front

Casing

Waist

Waist

10 in.

9 in.

Actual length + 1 in. to 2 in. extra

Measure the hips at the widest point.

Measure the pattern between the stitching lines, allowing for a seam allowance. Compare the pattern the same distance from the waistline that you measure on your body.

Fleece with spandex may require adjustments in the pattern for the best use of the stretch. Though many patterns designed for spandex fabrics use 10% to 20% of the stretch available in the fabric, garments made from stretch fleece fit better when only 3% to 5% of the stretch is used. Above, the fit has been adjusted on the pattern on the right to reflect the 3% to 5% stretch.

means they have what I call "negative ease." That is, if your body measures 40 in. at the hips, a pattern for leggings that uses spandex fabric with 100% stretch might measure only 32 in. at the hips, removing 8 in. of ease (giving a negative 8-in. ease) and utilizing 20% of the stretch. Though the fabric has 100% stretch available in the crossgrain and the straight grain in unbonded stretch fleece, it seems stiffer and less flexible if it's stretched more than a small percentage. Therefore, I prefer to use only 3% to 5% of the stretch. For a 40-in. hip measurement, I would use no more than a negative 2-in. ease, or a flat-pattern measurement of 38 in. (see the illustration on p. 47).

Spandex garments should not be shorter than your actual length. When the garment is worn and is using the crossgrain stretch around the body, the garment actually becomes shorter unless it has some support over the length. Stirrups are used to compensate for this shortening by pulling the garment from the heel to the waist (or the shoulder as the case may be). If you are making stirrup pants with a waistband, the waistband needs to be firm enough to stay up when in use (1½-in. nonroll sport elastic works well). If you aren't using stirrups and are worried about the garment being too short, add a few inches when cutting out, then trim the excess after trying on the partially complete garment.

Fitting with bonded fabrics

Bonded fleeces and pile have less flexibility than unbonded fabrics (see pp. 12-13). Those with spandex have some give to the fabric but should not be made with a negative ease. Bonded fleece with spandex should be made close to the actual body measurements, with extra shaping to accommodate the movement of the sport the garment is made for. An extra-heavy stretch fabric might be inserted at strategic areas for greater flexibility, such as a back-waist insert or side-seam inserts from the underarm or waist to the lower hip (see the illustration below).

For downhill ski bibs or one-piece racing suits, add extra length to the front leg in the side seam at the knee area and shorten the back-knee area (see the illustration on the facing page). When sewing the pieces together, the extra length at the front is eased in by stretching the

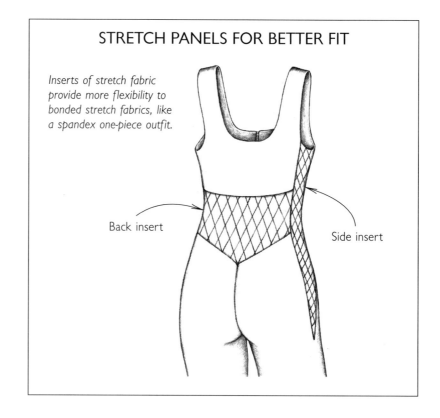

STRETCH PANELS FOR BETTER FIT

Inserts of stretch fabric provide more flexibility to bonded stretch fabrics, like a spandex one-piece outfit.

Back insert

Side insert

Chapter Three

48

BUILDING A BETTER FIT FOR A DOWNHILL RACING SUIT

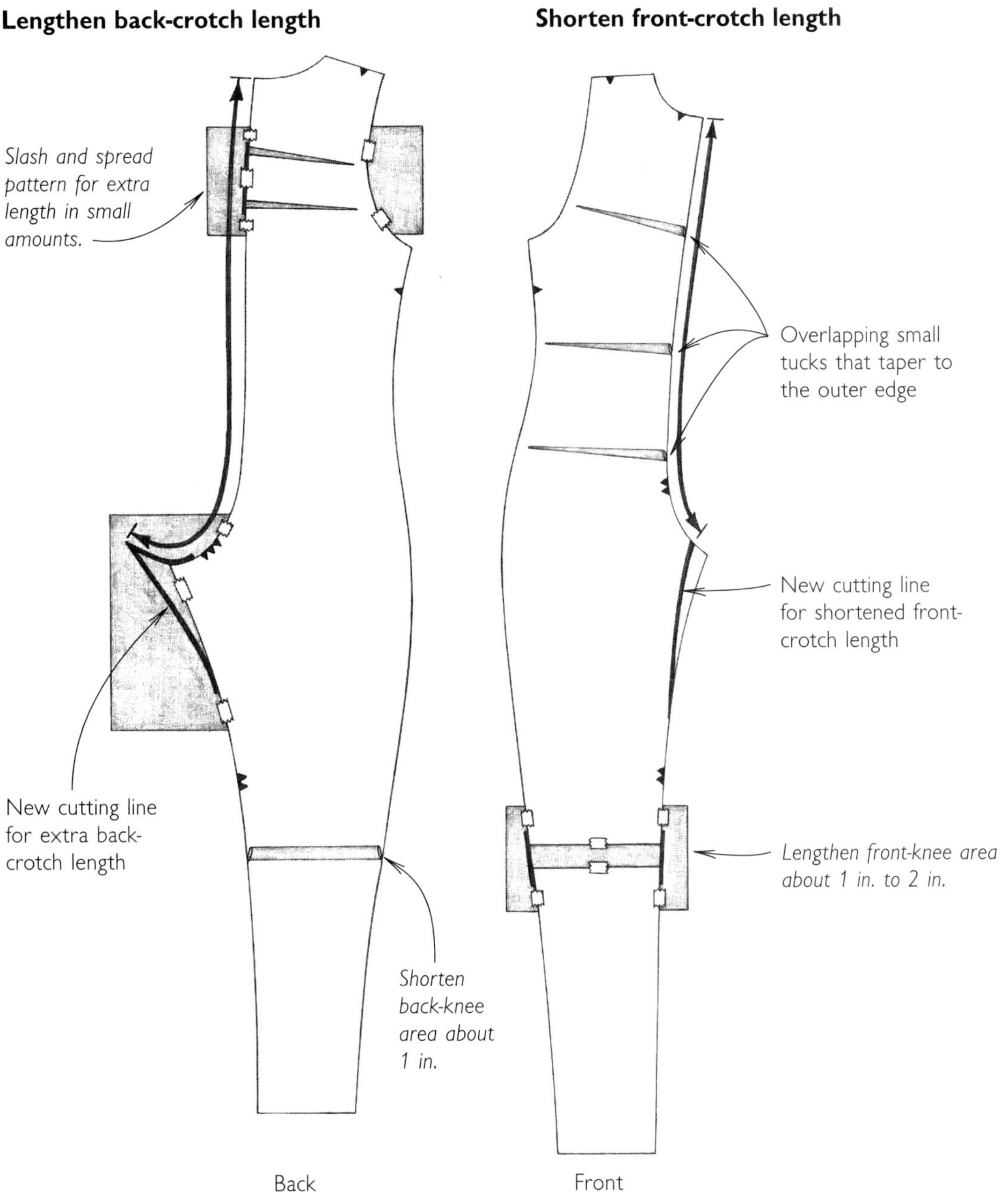

Lengthen back-crotch length

Slash and spread pattern for extra length in small amounts.

New cutting line for extra back-crotch length

Shorten front-crotch length

Overlapping small tucks that taper to the outer edge

New cutting line for shortened front-crotch length

Lengthen front-knee area about 1 in. to 2 in.

Shorten back-knee area about 1 in.

Back

Front

A ski racing suit can be made from a body-suit pattern with alterations that enhance fit for an aerodynamic "tuck" position. By adjusting the crotch point forward, adding length to the front-knee area, and taking length out of the back-knee area, the garment can be shaped to fit the position of the body as it folds forward at the waist and the knees fold back into a deep sit.

seamline of the back-knee area while stitching (work with the shorter piece on top and the longer piece on the bed of the machine). The back-crotch length should be longer than the front-crotch length. These modifications make it more comfortable for the wearer to be in the "tuck" position required in skiing.

PREPARING THE FABRIC FOR CUTTING

It usually isn't necessary to prewash synthetic fleeces. However, if you have any doubts about the fabric, be safe rather than sorry—wash and dry it ahead of time. As more and more natural fibers (which tend to shrink and are weaker than synthetics) are incorporated into fleece and pile fabrics, it will become important to prewash those fabrics according to the cleaning method you will be using with the completed garment.

Examine the right side of the fabric carefully. It's easy to miss flaws until they end up on the front of your jacket collar. If you find any suspect areas, put a piece of masking tape over the area so it's easier to identify and lay your pattern around that area. Lay the fabric on a flat surface to

see if there are any edges stretched out of shape that you need to work around. It may also help to hold the fabric up to the light, which will show any distortion of the knitted core that isn't obvious from the surface but will show up in the way the garment hangs when you wear it. This situation usually comes up with end pieces from a remnant or flat-fold table, but, as I mentioned in Chapter 1, fabric stores sometimes get flawed goods that a manufacturer rejected.

You may want to mark the right side of the fabric for convenience while sewing, but you can easily remind yourself during the sewing process by pulling a cut edge to see which way it curls. If the grain runs vertical through the pattern pieces, the fabric

will curl to the right side on vertical edges and to the wrong side on the crossgrain (see the photo below).

CUTTING OUT THE PATTERN

Many patterns include a diagram for cutting out that may or may not be useful. If you are using a fabric with a design that follows a particular nap direction (see p. 26) or that needs to be matched at the seams like a directional design (see pp. 26-27), or if you are just a *smidge* short of the required yardage, the diagram may not be of much help. This means that you may have to create your own pattern layout.

As you lay out your pattern pieces, fabric weights

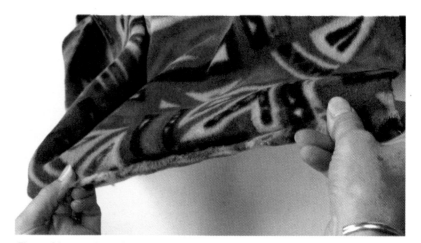

Fleece fabric curls to the right side on the selvage and on all vertical edges.

may be useful on thinner, lighter-weight fleeces, but thick fleece and pile will cause the weights to distort the edges of the paper pattern by sinking into the pile. The results will be more exact if you pin, as long as you are careful not to distort the paper pattern.

Cutting tools

A rotary cutter can be used with a single layer of light-weight to mid-weight fleece (especially when cutting strips for cording or binding), but heavier-weight fleeces are harder to cut accurately. When using a rotary cutter, trim excess paper from the pattern outside of the cutting line because the rotary cutter will chew up the pattern if you try to cut through both the pattern and the fabric.

A disadvantage to using a rotary cutter with fleece and pile is that as it cuts, it forces fleece and pile fibers into the cutting mat, making the mat less effective. To clean the fibers out of the mat, I use the side of my large clear ruler to scrape the fibers out. Another disadvantage of synthetic fleece is that it dulls the blade of the rotary cutter more quickly, so you'll need to use a blade sharpener frequently.

Sharp scissors make a big difference in how easy it is to cut synthetic fleece and pile. Scissors that are dull or have nicks in them make you feel as if you would have better luck with your teeth.

Cutting techniques

Here are some simple techniques for cutting out the pattern that will make the process easier.

- Cut only one layer at a time, especially with heavier-weight fleeces and pile.
- Make a full pattern piece from a pattern piece that has a foldline by tracing the pattern on tissue and taping the two halves together. Or when cutting out, make a clip in the fabric at the top and bottom of the pattern piece at the foldline after cutting one side, then flip the pattern piece over and reposition it at the foldline to continue cutting.
- Cut notches as clips in the seam allowance for easy matching, but don't use clips where there is no seam allowance (butted seams, flatlock seams, corded edges, etc).
- Cut pile fabrics on the wrong side. By cutting the backing fabric only, you can eliminate a lot of the mess that loose fibers create (see the photo below). Trim thick pile away from seam allowances, but leave the backing fabric if you want to topstitch through all layers.

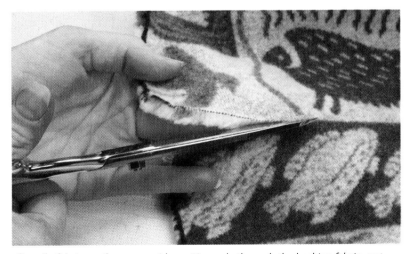

Cut pile fabric on the wrong side, cutting only through the backing fabric, not through the pile.

SEWING TIPS & TECHNIQUES

What follows are tips for general sewing options that you will find useful in your "toolbox." You may also find these tips helpful for other types of fabrics and combinations of fabrics. Some techniques may be specific to certain types of machines, but I have tried to include methods that will work even if you have a sewing machine that is exclusively straight stitch.

Some techniques duplicate manufacturers' methods of construction. These techniques are typically quick and easy, with somewhat pre-

dictable results. Other techniques have been developed from experimentation and play. You can develop your own ideas–don't feel locked into doing things the way they are shown here. Fabrics, technology, and styles change, so use this information as a foundation for moving with the changes.

These techniques generally apply to fleece and pile fabrics with knit construction, but they will work with woven fleece as well. However, if there is reference to the stretch of the fabric, you may

assume woven fleece is not applicable to that particular technique.

You can minimize frustration in all of your sewing by making samples of the techniques you intend to use. Different fabric characteristics yield different results using the same technique. Samples save time and the wear and tear on the fabric that ripping out produces.

Construction and finishing techniques give character and structural support to a fleece garment.

In addition to the general sewing tips, we'll look at more specific techniques relating to seams, edge and hem finishes, pocket options, closures, drawcords and casings, zippers, and lining.

FEEDING THE FABRIC

The bulk of the fabric is always of special concern on heavier-weight fleeces. It affects the way the fabric feeds through the machine and can cause uneven seams. To make sure the seams come out evenly, you should pin the seamline every 3 in. to 4 in.

Stretching all layers slightly from front to back under the presser foot while stitching flattens the fabric some and helps to keep seam threads from breaking. Sometimes compressing the fabric with your fingers along the seamline as it goes under the presser foot helps the fabric feed evenly (see the photo below). You may also find a walking foot useful with heavier-weight fleeces.

On a serger, the differential feed should be used with fleece and pile. The heavier the fabric, the higher the setting on the differential feed. For heavyweight fleece, you

can turn the differential feed up to the maximum and increase the pressure on the presser foot to get a nice flat seam. For sergers without a differential feed, increasing the foot pressure may be counterproductive because it can cause the fabric to feed unevenly, so you may want to lessen it.

The serger stitch length may vary according to the type of seaming method you are using, but generally the heavier the fabric, the longer the stitch should be to prevent rippled seams.

Compress the fabric with your fingers to help it feed evenly.

Making Secure, Flat Seams

When using the longer stitch lengths required for sewing with fleece and pile, it is very important to secure the beginning and end of each stitching line with a back tack (unless it's a basting stitch or you are otherwise advised), or the end of the seam will immediately begin to loosen up. Zigzag stitches can be secured by starting the seam with a few straight stitches with a back tack and then changing the width setting to begin the zigzag. Serged seams should have an inch of the thread tail left in place until that edge is sewn down or to another edge. Flatlock seams are especially susceptible to pulling

out, so I always topstitch through the flattened seam before cutting the thread tails off.

If a seam is rippling, it is because there is too much thread in the fabric at the seamline. To fix this, make the stitch length longer so that less thread is in the fabric. This applies to both straight-stitch and overlocked seams. If the thread is breaking when the seam is pulled, stretch the fabric layers more while stitching and/or loosen the needle thread tension.

To avoid uneven seams when stitching with two different types of fabric, keep the fabric with the most give (stretch) on the bed of the machine and the more stable fabric on the top (see the photo

below). This allows the feed dogs to do the work of getting the more stubborn fabric through the machine. Layering fabric this way is also important when applying zippers (stitch with the stable zipper tape on top). With some techniques, like stretch binding, it may not be practical to follow this suggestion because it would place the bulk of the garment to the right side of the needle and make it more difficult to manipulate the edges. But the smoother texture of the nylon stretch binding and the stretching process help the fabric slide under the presser foot more easily.

When stitching two different fabric types together, the fabric with the most bulk and/or stretch should be on the bottom.

TENSION

Thread tension on your serger or sewing machine may need to be changed to accommodate the give in fleece fabric. If the seam is too tight, check that the thread is feeding from the spool, that the machine is threaded properly, and that the stitch length is not too short. If these things are correct, then try loosening the upper thread tension. You can also use woolly nylon thread in the bobbin to add ease to the seam.

SEAMS

Seams are the foundation of a successful garment. They define its shape and determine its capacity to hold up to everyday use. Fleece and pile garments often need seams that can stretch or have some give. Many seams work well when sewing in fleece and pile, but here are the ones that I use most often. You may find others that fit your own style of sewing.

Straight-stitch seam

A straight stitch produces a flat, straight seam that is useful on its own or with topstitching on all weights of fabric. In fleece and pile, the stitch length should be set at a medium to a long setting to avoid rippling seams. Testing seams will help you determine the correct length for a specific fabric. A straight-stitch seam without topstitching can be stitched with any width seam allowance, but to reduce bulk, the seam allowance should be trimmed close to the seamline (about ⅛ in.). This type of seam is less stiff than a topstitched seam and works nicely for better drape in garments made with lightweight pile and microfleece. Extra stretch can be added to a straight-stitch seam by setting the width of the stitch to a slight zigzag.

This is the easiest and best seam for very thick piles, but you should trim the pile from the seam allowance before using the straight stitch (see the photo below).

Topstitched seam

Topstitching gives sharper definition to fabric that can't be easily ironed or steamed into place. All weights of fleece and pile can use a topstitched seam, although stretch types of fleece should be stretched while stitching to avoid break-

Trim pile from the edge before stitching the seam.

ing seam threads. Topstitching uses a medium to long stitch length, and the heavier the weight of the fabric, the longer the stitch.

For a double-edged top-stitched seam, make a regular straight-stitch seam, using seam allowances wide enough to underlay the topstitching. Finger-press the seam allowances open, then topstitch from the right side along both sides of the seam (see the photo above). The distance is up to you, but the topstitching should go through the seam allowance.

A false flat-fell topstitched seam requires only one pass of a topstitching line to secure it. After stitching the first seamline using a ⅝-in. seam allowance, trim one side

of the seam allowance, fold the remaining seam allowance across the seamline, and topstitch through all layers ⅜ in. from the seamline. If possible, stitch in the same direction on the topstitching pass as on the first stitching pass. This will help prevent twisting of the seam allowance. If desired, after topstitching, trim any seam allowance that extends beyond the topstitching.

With a sleeve or narrow pant leg, it is difficult to topstitch in a space that is so narrow. In these instances, I topstitch the side seam up to the armscye and then trim both the seam allowances of the undersleeve seam if it's too difficult to topstitch.

Zigzag seam

A medium-width and medium-length zigzag stitch will also work for a seam on most fleece and pile weights, but it is less attractive on lighter-weight fabrics, where the seam is easier to see. It is a thicker seam than a straight-stitch seam, so it's not as easy to topstitch a neat seam after trimming. It is a good substitute for a serged seam when some stretch or ease is desired on stretchy fleece and pile. A double needle produces a zigzag stitch with the bobbin thread and can be used in the same way.

The seam allowance can be just wide enough to catch both edges of the stitch; or a seam allowance that is wider than the stitch can be used, and the excess seam allowance can be trimmed off after stitching.

Seams with trim

Manufacturers use a straight stitch in combination with narrow trim to join two edges. It is often seen at the neck, where the collar is joined to the body, but I have used microfleece strips and a version of this technique in the pile coat on p. 15, with all the seams on the right side of the coat. All weights of fleece and pile can be used with this technique, but the weight and width of the trim should relate to the weight of the fabric. The heavier the fabric, the heavier and wider the trim should be. Stitch length should be a medium to long stitch setting. The seam

allowance is variable, but it is easier for trimming if it is ⅜ in. or wider.

When preparing the seam, if the rights sides are together, the trim and seam will show on the wrong side of the finished garment. If the wrong sides are together, then the trim will show on the right side of the garment.

Place the trim over the seam allowance area so the inside edge will be caught in the stitching line. Trim away the seam allowances, lay the joined pieces flat, fold the trim over the stitching line (keeping the work flat underneath to avoid puckers), and stitch the remaining edge through the trim and fabric.

On a collar application, use a narrow, matte-finish trim instead of satin ribbon, which

is less comfortable. Stitch the seam so that the second stitched edge is stitched to the straighter collar piece instead of to the curved edge of the body piece.

Butted and lapped seams

There are many times that a butted seam may be useful. Areas that need to be very flat, such as the crotch padding in cycling shorts, benefit from this seam. Most weights of fleece and pile can be used with this seam, but mid-weight to heavyweight fabrics look best. The zigzag-stitch settings should be at the widest, with a medium to long length. There is no seam allowance in this stitch, so trim them before stitching.

To make a butted seam, two cut edges are placed side

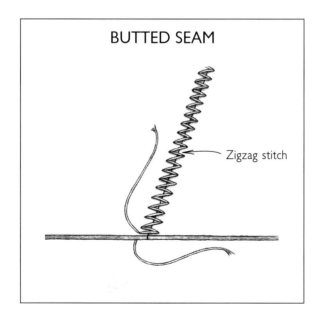

BUTTED SEAM

Zigzag stitch

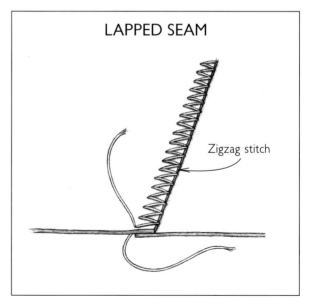

LAPPED SEAM

Zigzag stitch

by side with any necessary matching points lined up and zigzagged to catch both pieces of fabric in the stitching line (see the left illustration on the facing page). Sometimes piecing odd bits of fleece in a crazy quilt style creates a wonderful effect with a butted seam.

A lapped seam is similar to the butted seam and used in the same way. However, the lapped seam requires a seam allowance half the width of the stitch used. One cut edge is lapped over another and stitched in place with a zigzag or other decorative stitch (see the right illustration on the facing page). These two stitching techniques are terrific for painlessly piecing curved edges together. I've used them when I didn't have enough of a particularly wonderful fabric to cut out all my pattern pieces. I color-blocked sleeves with a coordinating print border by using a lapped seam, and the results were great.

Serged seams

The serger has the capacity for a naturally stretchy seam, but with the bulk of the fleece and pile there are some features and seam types that will be more useful than others. As I mentioned before, the differential feed is very helpful in feeding the fabric through the machine evenly. The thicker the fabric, the higher the setting for the differential feed. In conjunction with the differential feed, increase the pressure on the presser foot. As with most stitching on fleece and pile, keep the stitch length on the long side to avoid rippling.

With lighter-weight fleeces, a four-thread serged seam can be used alone or with a top-stitching line ⅛ in. from the seamline through all layers. If the fabric contains spandex, a three-thread stitch will give greater stretch with a lower differential setting.

Flatlock seam

The two-thread flatlock stitch is one of the most under-utilized seams of the serger. Lightweight to mid-weight knit fabrics of all types benefit from this seam type. It is stitched with the wrong sides together, then pulled flat to produce a seam with cut edges enclosed in the stitching. This reduces chafing in close-fitting garments. A flatlock seam is an excellent choice for spandex activewear.

There are no seam allowances necessary for this seam, so cut them off from the pattern pieces before you cut out your fabric. Or you can cut out your fabric as usual and trim away the width of the seam allowance.

Your machine manual has general instructions for setting up two-thread or three-thread stitching (with the needle position at the widest setting) and for the tension settings for the needle and looper. In general, the needle tension will be as loose as possible or out of the tension dial totally, and the lower looper will be at a medium level. To see what works best, you should make samples using different stitch lengths, differential feed settings, and even different looper threads for contrast stitching.

Before you start stitching, check the cut edges of the garment pieces, making sure there are no gouges or bulges at the fabric edge. Imperfection in the cut edge will show up in the finished stitching line. When stitching, guide the cut edges through the machine halfway between the needle and the cutting blade (see the photo on p. 60). The fabric will open inside the stitching with less bulk. After the fabric is folded and finger-pressed flat, I topstitch a stabilizing stitch through the center of the flatlock seam to secure the threads crossing the joined fabric and to help it lie flat. The threads crossing the seam are like a floating thread that can be easily snagged if not stitched down in this manner.

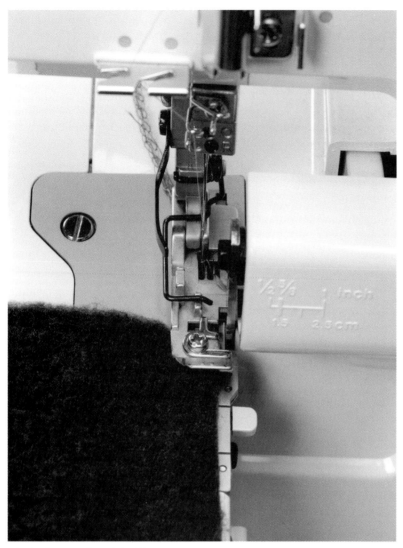

Guide the cut edge of the fabric through the serger halfway between the needle and the cutting blade.

FINISHING EDGES AND HEMS

A self-fabric facing or a simple rolled hem is a quick finish for thinner fabrics, but fleece requires consideration for its bulk and knit construction. Edge finishing can be a very creative aspect of sewing with fleece and pile. Some of the edge finishes that follow give a distinctive look by outlining the shape of the garment and emphasizing the design line. Others are subtle, softly finishing the garment in a less obtrusive way. Each finishing option is a design tool that can add to the statement of the garment. As always, you should make a sample on the fashion fabric to visualize the effect the edge finish produces.

Standard facings and hems

The double thickness of a facing and/or hem may be just the look you want for your garment (see Stabilizers on p. 41 for interfacing information). For facing seams, the seam allowances should be graded close to the stitching line so that it is easier to topstitch the edge (see the illustration on the facing page). Hems should be stitched without rolling the cut edge under (as with a rolled hem). A straight or zigzag stitch with a single or double needle can be used to stitch the hem. If you want a more finished look on the inside, bind the cut edge of the hem allowance with a bias binding, then straight-stitch or hand-stitch the binding in place.

A machine-stitched blind hem will also give satisfactory results on lightweight to

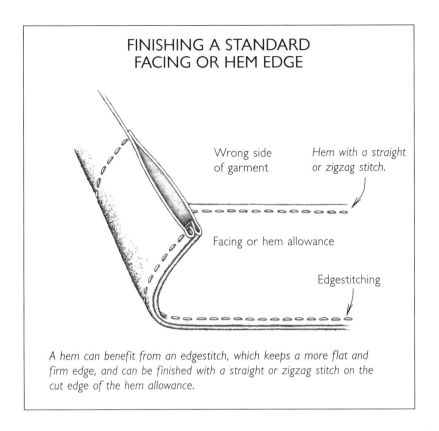

FINISHING A STANDARD FACING OR HEM EDGE

Wrong side of garment

Hem with a straight or zigzag stitch.

Facing or hem allowance

Edgestitching

A hem can benefit from an edgestitch, which keeps a more flat and firm edge, and can be finished with a straight or zigzag stitch on the cut edge of the hem allowance.

mid-weight fleece and pile, but thicker types are hard to get under the presser foot.

A facing made from a woven companion fabric is an excellent alternative to a double thickness of fleece. The pattern for the Hong Kong vest pictured on p. 38 had a cut-on facing around the bottom and the exposed side edges that was replaced with a facing. The existing edge was changed by drawing a new cutting line one seam-allowance width outside of the existing foldline (which will be the new cutting line). The separate facing pattern was made by tracing the new

cutting and stitching lines on a separate piece of pattern paper (see the illustration on p. 62). The desired width of the new facing is then drawn, adding a small hem allowance for turning under when stitching it in place. The facing on the vest armscye was also made from the same triblend fabric so that all the edges were sharply defined when finished with an edgestitch. The facings didn't need to be interfaced, but I wanted to prevent boardiness (stiffness), so I chose a lightweight, flexible interfacing. For even feed, the woven fabric was kept on top during stitching.

The Haiku jacket shown with the Hong Kong vest (see p. 38) has the same triblend fabric underlining the front lapel, with a slightly heavier interfacing applied to the triblend. Much of the detail stitching was done to the single layer of fleece before the stable facing was applied. To secure the two layers together, it was necessary to stitch with the fleece layer on top to follow the stitched design. To prevent the two layers from torquing, they were pinned together at short intervals, and the fleece was compressed in front of the presser

MAKING A SEPARATE FACING PATTERN

New facing stitching line

Original pattern foldline

New facing cutting line

New cutting line with seam allowance for facing and garment edge

Original pattern cut-on hem

A corner from the hem of a vest pattern with a cut-on hem can be used to make a separate facing pattern. To make the new facing pattern, trace the fold of the hem as the new stitching line, measure and draw the desired width of the new facing (plus its hem allowance), and add the seam allowance outside the new stitching line. The width of the seam allowance outside of the new stitching line will determine the new cutting line for both pieces.

foot. (A walking foot may also be very useful in this situation.)

Borders as edges or hems

Another hem option is to apply a trim or fleece border to the wrong side of the cut edge. The hem is then turned to the right side of the garment and topstitched to finish (see the illustration on the facing page).

Topstitching

Topstitching is a valuable tool for edges as well as for seams when sewing on fleece and pile. It turns a thick, mushy edge into a firm, more defined edge. Extra rows of topstitching can add dimension and firmness to the edge (see the illustration on p. 64).

Though you can use a multiple needle (double or triple) for topstitching, for edges I prefer to use a single needle and stitch each row separately. It makes the stitching identical on the right and wrong sides of the garment and avoids having to adjust the tension to keep the multiple needle from forming a pintuck. When stitching, keep the presser foot fully on the fabric, if possible, and then offset the needle to make it easier to stitch (see the sidebar on p. 64). Also, consider using some of the attachments that come with your machine for making topstitching easier.

Cut edges

A terrific advantage to working with fleece is that it does not fray. This creates many options for edge finishes that are not possible with other fabrics. Lightweight, thinner microfleeces can be cut with

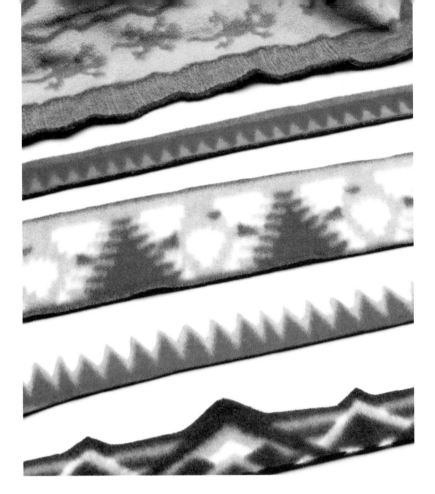

As a hem or edge option, borders can be cut from print fabrics and stitched to the edge of the garment.

USING A BORDER AS AN EDGE OR HEM

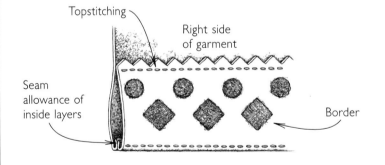

Topstitching

Right side of garment

Seam allowance of inside layers

Border

Adding a border is similar to adding a trim. Stitch the right side of the border to the wrong-side edge of the garment, trim the seam allowance, and then turn to the right side and topstitch.

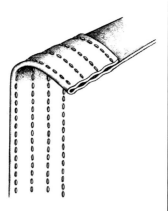

TOPSTITCHING THE EDGE

Single rows of topstitching add a crisp, firm edge without being stiff.

Offsetting the Needle for Uneven or Thick Edges

When stitching in multiple layers of a fabric as thick as many fleeces and piles, the problem of the presser foot riding unevenly on the fabric arises. If two layers of mid-weight to heavyweight fleece are being fed under the middle of the foot, the foot will not ride evenly on the fabric and will tend to push the fabric to one side. This is the perfect reason to use the needle-offsetting option on most zigzag machines.

Offsetting the needle to one side allows you to move the cut edges of the fabric so that the presser foot rides fully on the fabric, and the fabric feeds through easily. When topstitching, I prefer to set the edge of the presser foot at the seamline and offset the needle to the desired distance. This makes it easier to stitch at a consistent distance from the seam.

pinking shears along edges that would otherwise have to be hemmed.

You can create a unique cut edge by using a template, tracing around the edge of the pattern onto the fabric, and then cutting the pattern from the fabric with sharp scissors. Printed borders may have part of the pattern cut out before stitching to another fabric to reveal the bottom fabric through the cut border. Your cutting pattern should be tested on a sample first, with some stress put on the sample to make sure it won't curl significantly in the crossgrain and small pattern designs won't pull off from the fabric. When using these techniques, you should trim

away seam and hem allowances and check your pattern to be sure you are cutting off the correct amount.

Fringe

Fringed edges can be cut on the crossgrain (cutting lines parallel with the grain). If you cut fringe across the grain (cutting lines parallel with the crossgrain), the fringe will curl if pulled. You can experiment with the width to find the best results for the weight of the fabric used—¼ in. to ⅜ in. is about right for most fleeces. Remember, pile fabrics should be cut from the backing side, and the fringe kept a little bit wider because there is more vertical stretch to it, and it may have a slight curl anyway. (For more information on fringe see p. 108.)

Decorative stitches

Decorative stitching can be added to a cut edge by hand or by machine. Home-decor items like pillows and throws are being manufactured with a simple blanket-stitch edge, and they command a relatively high price for the small amount of time required to finish them. Simple cutout appliqués from fleece can be stitched on with a blanket stitch to quickly create dimension on a vest, jacket, or throw.

The long edges of a blanket can be stitched with cord made from a narrow crossgrain strip of fleece. The fleece strip has been pulled taut to lose most of its stretch. The fleece edge to be stitched should be prepoked with an awl or stitched with a leather needle to create a hole large enough for the fleece cord to pass through. (Be sure the eye of the needle is large enough for the cord.) Use the blanket stitch for a dramatic edge with a contrasting color or to add the effect of a traditional blanket coat. It adds minimal bulk but is highly decorative (see the illustration above).

Many machines have a blanket stitch in their arsenal

HAND-SEWN BLANKET STITCH

½ in. wide

½ in. deep

The blanket stitch creates a colorful, textural edge without a lot of bulk when stitched with fleece cord in a contrasting color. With hand stitching, the stitch can be much larger than a machine-stitched edge.

of decorative stitches. This is a good option for the thinner, lightweight fleeces. On heavyweight fleeces, the thread may disappear in the thick fiber. If you're using heavyweight fleece, check your machine manual for other edge-finish options. More-open stitches work best; satin-stitching will leave a rippled edge.

Edgestitching on a serger can make use of the several decorative threads available.

The decorative threads should be used in the loopers only and edgestitched with a shorter stitch length for a more solid edge of color.

Binding

Though you may not be used to making edge bindings, you'll soon find that they can be almost as quick as a rolled hem and have infinitely more possibilities. As you will see, bindings can be used to sim-

General Binding Tips

Many people are intimidated by the binding process for fear that the results will be twisted, bulky, and look homemade, not hand-crafted. But with the help of the tips here, you'll be using binding on most of your projects.

- When binding a curve, slightly stretch the main fabric at the seamline to straighten the curve while stitching. This will ease in the seamline of the binding so that it will lie flat.

- When possible, apply the binding before the seams are joined adjacent to the bound edge. For example, a sleeve hem edge can be bound before the underarm seam is sewn.

- To stitch a seam through a finished binding, start stitching in the middle of the binding, then backstitch to the edge of the binding and begin stitching forward (see the illustration at right). This will help prevent the binding from stretching out of place. Finger-press the seam allowance open at the binding and bar-tack across the seam at the binding on the right side of the work. Trim the seam allowances close to the bar tack.

- When binding needs to be finished at the end, wrap ½ in. of binding to the other side of the work at either end of the bound section (see the top illustration on the facing page). Pull the ends over to the other side when wrapping and then follow the instructions for binding on pp. 65 and 68. This technique finishes the end of the work neatly. If the ends are difficult to keep tight to the work, leave the ½-in. tail loose over the end of the work while stitching the first pass, then wrap the tail to the other side and stitch just the tail while pulling it firmly over the end of the work. Continue as directed for the binding technique you have chosen.

- When the two ends of the binding meet, as at the lower edge of a pullover, fold up the cut end when starting the stitching line. When ending the stitching line, continue the binding over the beginning fold for ½ in. before cutting off. As you fold the binding to the right side, the cut end will be enclosed within the binding (see the bottom illustration on the facing page). For double-layer binding, fold the beginning end before folding the binding lengthwise and then start stitching.

- If the binding continues around a corner, make mitered corners instead of the folded-over ends shown in the top illustration on the facing page. Follow the instructions on pp. 104-105 for folded or stitched mitered corners.

SEAM THROUGH A FINISHED BINDING

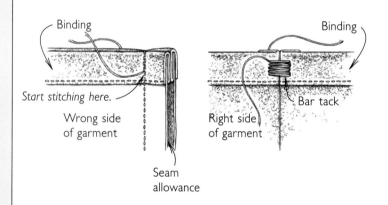

Binding

Start stitching here.

Wrong side of garment

Seam allowance

Binding

Bar tack

Right side of garment

Avoid stretching the binding out of shape by starting to stitch in the middle of the binding, stitching backward then forward from the outer edge of the binding.

Open the seam and bar-tack the binding from the right side before trimming the excess seam allowance from the back side.

SMOOTH END FINISH FOR BINDING

1 *Wrap a ½-in. length of binding to the back side at the beginning or end of the work on the first pass of stitching. Pin the layers in place to make sure the excess is as tight as possible around the end.*

2 *Wrap the binding to the right side. With this method, the ends are prefolded.*

3 *The binding is then finished with topstitching, and the ends have only folds visible.*

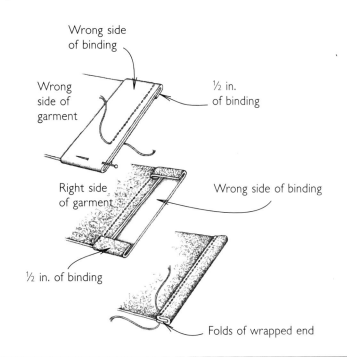

Wrong side of binding

Wrong side of garment

½ in. of binding

Wrong side of binding

Right side of garment

½ in. of binding

Folds of wrapped end

BINDING WHEN TWO ENDS MEET

1 *Where the ends of the binding meet, begin by folding ½ in. at the cut end of the binding back on itself. Stitch around the garment, securing the folded end with the first stitches and overlapping the binding and stitching at the beginning fold.*

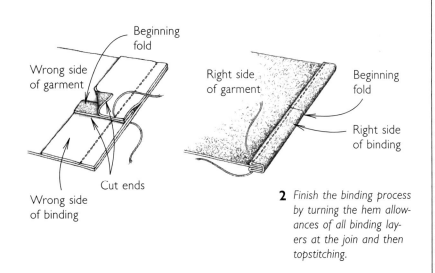

Beginning fold

Wrong side of garment

Wrong side of binding

Cut ends

Right side of garment

Beginning fold

Right side of binding

2 *Finish the binding process by turning the hem allowances of all binding layers at the join and then topstitching.*

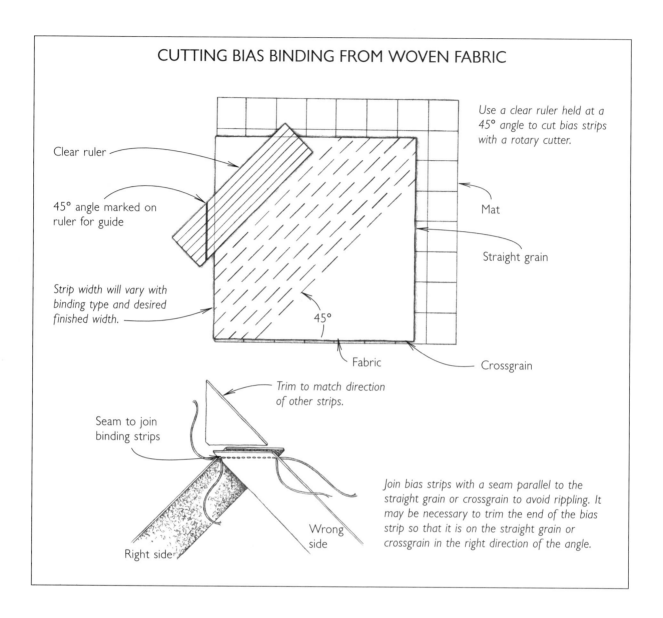

CUTTING BIAS BINDING FROM WOVEN FABRIC

Clear ruler

45° angle marked on ruler for guide

Strip width will vary with binding type and desired finished width.

Use a clear ruler held at a 45° angle to cut bias strips with a rotary cutter.

Mat

Straight grain

45°

Fabric

Crossgrain

Trim to match direction of other strips.

Seam to join binding strips

Join bias strips with a seam parallel to the straight grain or crossgrain to avoid rippling. It may be necessary to trim the end of the bias strip so that it is on the straight grain or crossgrain in the right direction of the angle.

Wrong side

Right side

ply finish an edge, to elasticize an edge, to emphasize an edge, or to hold a drawcord.

The width of the binding is determined by the method of binding. Woven bias-cut binding should be cut on the true bias at a 45° angle from the crossgrain and straight grain (see the illustration above). A rotary cutter, mat, and clear ruler are useful for cutting bias from woven fabrics, fleece binding, or stretch binding strips (see the photo on the facing page). With these tools the cutting is so fast that I cut several more strips than I need and save a stash of binding to select from on impulse. If you don't have these tools, mark cutting lines with a straightedge and a chalk wheel before cutting with sharp scissors.

Binding with spandex
Binding with spandex-blend fabrics has become popular since the introduction of fleece garments in ready-to-wear. It is an easy process but may

require some fine-tuning on sample fabric to get exactly the effect you want.

If you are looking for a spandex-blend fabric to create a gathered-stretch edge, select a fabric that has 100% stretch in the crossgrain so that you can cut the binding across the width, using less yardage. Nylon/spandex blends with a 100% crossgrain stretch are often used in swimwear and cycling wear, and they have the durability to hold up in fleece and pile outerwear. If you don't like the shine of the face of the fabric, use the wrong side, which is usually a matte finish.

You should try not to piece two sections of binding together because it's hard not to get a lumpy spot at the join. Spandex-blend fabrics usually come in 60-in. widths, and it would be highly unusual to need pieces longer than that. If you do need to join binding sections, try not to stretch the fabric as you stitch, use a longer stitch, and trim the seam allowance close to the stitching line.

Spandex-blend fabrics are also useful for flat binding. As you stitch, feed through the fabric and binding at a 1:1 ratio while gently stretching them together. Lingerie-weight spandex fabrics are excellent for this technique, but colors are limited.

The weight of the spandex will have a lot to do with the method of binding you choose and the results you get. Make note of the suggested fabric types and weights for the different binding applications that follow.

Stitch-in-the-ditch binding

The stitch-in-the-ditch binding is useful for both flat and gathered-stretch binding. To make this binding, cut the binding four times the desired finished width. Using a medium to long stitch length, sew the binding on the garment edge with the right sides together and the long cut edges matching (see the illustration on p. 70). Stitch one binding width from the cut edge. For a flat binding, hold both layers together and gently stretch them while stitching. For a gathered-stretch binding, position both layers

STITCH-IN-THE-DITCH BINDING

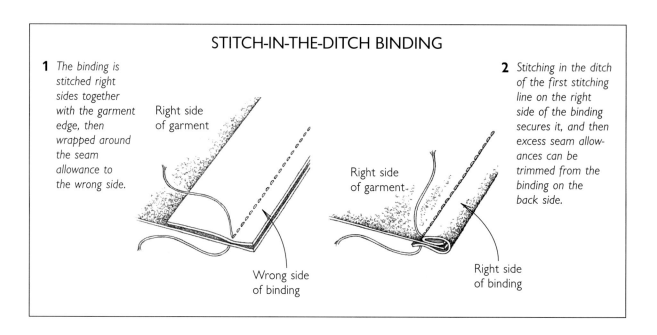

1 *The binding is stitched right sides together with the garment edge, then wrapped around the seam allowance to the wrong side.*

Right side of garment

Wrong side of binding

2 *Stitching in the ditch of the first stitching line on the right side of the binding secures it, and then excess seam allowances can be trimmed from the binding on the back side.*

Right side of garment

Right side of binding

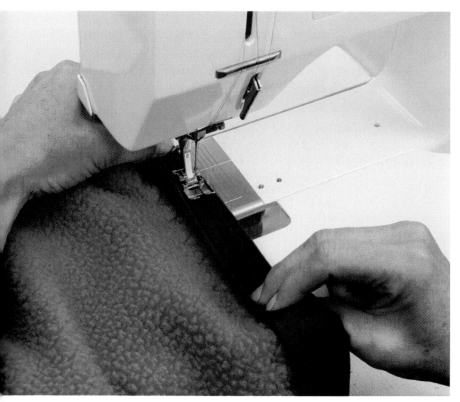

To stitch a gathered-stretch edge, position both layers under the presser foot and hold them firmly, stretching the binding first, then holding both layers firmly across the throat plate.

under the presser foot, stretch the binding only, then hold both layers firmly from front to back over the throat plate while stitching (see the photo at left). Once the binding is stitched, wrap it to the wrong side around the seam allowance (do not trim the fleece along the seam allowance). Seam allowances should be inside of the binding. Don't wrap the binding so far that it distorts the edge of fleece inside of the binding. Stitch in the ditch between the binding and the fleece. Trim excess binding away from the stitching line on the back of the work.

This method can be used for all different weights of fleece and bindings. Heavier-weight spandex fabrics can be used as a binding without the binding getting too bulky from multiple layers. Try to match heavier-weight materials (like fleece and binding) together and lighter-weight materials together.

The stitch-in-the-ditch method is ideal for using fleece as binding. Microfleece, which I used to bind the edge of the zipper tape in Maddie's coat, will produce a thin, soft profile. Mid-weight to heavy-weight fleeces are rounder and thicker, with more of a ropelike quality that can be emphasized by inserting a thin strip of glazed batting in the binding as it is top-stitched closed. If the binding fabric you have chosen has a tendency to twist when using other binding methods that switch stitching directions as the fabric is turned, this method may resolve the problem because you are stitching the same direction on both stitching passes.

Topstitched binding

Topstitched binding is the more common way to apply binding, normally using bias-cut woven fabric. The binding strips are cut four times the desired finished width of the binding. This technique is useful for binding made from bias-cut wovens, lightweight to mid-weight spandex fabrics, and lightweight fleeces (with a modification).

Bias strips from woven fabrics should be cut on the true bias from a fabric compatible to the fibers of the fleece or pile that you are working with. Synthetics designed for use in outerwear are a better choice for durability and wear than cotton. Synthetic wovens are notorious for fraying, but when they're cut on the bias, fraying shouldn't be a problem. Strips of bias should be joined on the straight grain or crossgrain (see the illustration on p. 68).

Place the right side of the binding to the wrong side of the garment edge. Straight-

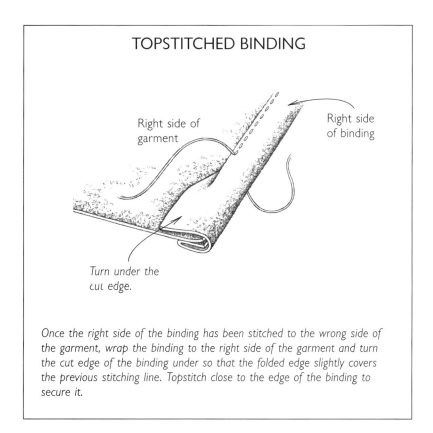

TOPSTITCHED BINDING

Right side of garment

Right side of binding

Turn under the cut edge.

Once the right side of the binding has been stitched to the wrong side of the garment, wrap the binding to the right side of the garment and turn the cut edge of the binding under so that the folded edge slightly covers the previous stitching line. Topstitch close to the edge of the binding to secure it.

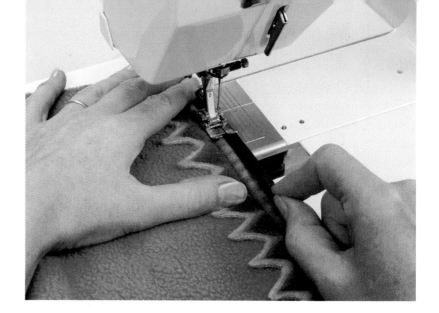

To finish binding, wrap the binding to the right side, roll under the cut edge, and topstitch through all layers near the binding edge while stretching all layers firmly.

Hand-stitch the finish on microfiber bias binding to prevent the binding from twisting.

stitch as explained previously for a flat or gathered-stretch binding. Wrap the binding to the right side and roll under the cut edge of the binding, placing the fold of binding slightly over the previous stitching line. Topstitch through all layers close to the folded binding edge (see illustration on p. 71 and the photo above).

I used this method with a microdenier woven fleece to bind the edges of Sarah's coat. The topstitching process pushed the binding fabric just enough to create a twist that I couldn't seem to eliminate with my machine, so I hand-stitched the top of the binding, and it looked terrific (see the photo at left)!

Another topstitched binding method that's a nice complement to fleece and pile is binding made from synthetic suede. It should be cut on the crossgrain two times the desired finished width. On the wrong side of the fleece, place the center foldline of the binding over the cut edge, wrong sides together, and edgestitch. Wrap the binding to the right side and topstitch, slightly overlapping the previous stitching line (see the illustrations at right).

When using a microfleece for a topstitched binding, I modify the process at the point of topstitching to the right side. Instead of rolling under the seam allowance, I cut it off and zigzag the cut edge over the first stitching line. Then I cut a narrow strip of fleece on the crossgrain (¼ in. to ⅜ in. wide) and stretch it firmly to create cording. I zigzag the cording over the previous zigzag (see the illustration on p. 74).

The same thing can be accomplished by stitching the cut edge and the cord in the same pass of the zigzag stitch. Some people may find it harder to manipulate all three edges at once. If there appears to be any puckering from the stretched cording, straight-stitch through the cording with a shorter stitch. By adding more thread to the stitching line, you can stretch it out. (For more information on cording, see the sidebar on p. 125.)

SINGLE-LAYER BINDING USING NONFRAYING FABRICS

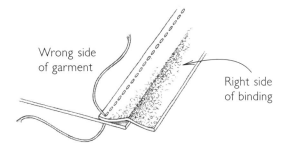

Wrong side of garment

Right side of binding

1 *Place the binding and the garment edge wrong sides together, with the foldline of the binding over the cut edge of the garment. Edgestitch close to the binding edge through both layers with a straight or zigzag stitch.*

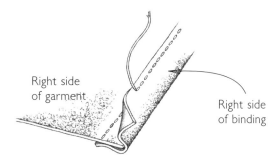

Right side of garment

Right side of binding

2 *Wrap the remaining edge of the binding to the right side of the garment. With the binding edge slightly overlapping the first stitching line, topstitch close to the binding through all layers to secure it.*

Zigzag the cording to finish the fleece binding for design details that enhance the Soutache effect (seen on Jo's Haiku jacket).

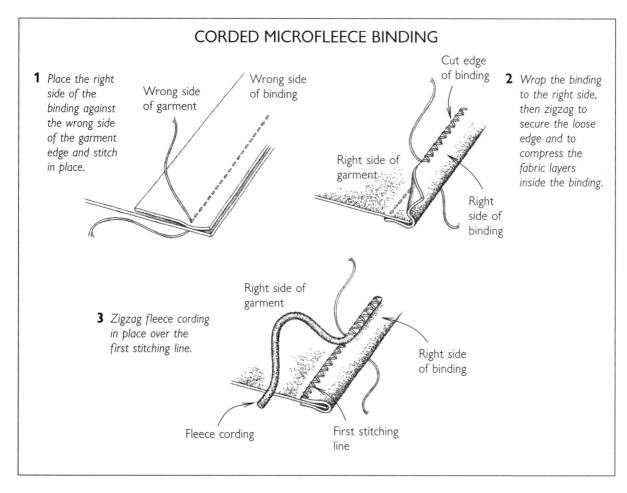

CORDED MICROFLEECE BINDING

1 *Place the right side of the binding against the wrong side of the garment edge and stitch in place.*

Wrong side of garment

Wrong side of binding

Cut edge of binding

Right side of garment

Right side of binding

2 *Wrap the binding to the right side, then zigzag to secure the loose edge and to compress the fabric layers inside the binding.*

3 *Zigzag fleece cording in place over the first stitching line.*

Right side of garment

Right side of binding

Fleece cording

First stitching line

Double-layer binding

Double-layer binding is used with lightweight spandex fabrics. Sometimes it's difficult to find exactly the right weight of fabric in the right color, but double-layer binding is perfect if the right color fabric is too lightweight because it actually firms up the binding fabric. Also, when you wrap the binding to the right side, you have a finished edge instead of fighting to roll under the seam allowance.

Cut the binding strips six times the desired finished binding width. Fold the binding lengthwise with the wrong sides together. Match the binding cut edges to the wrong side of the garment cut edge. Stitch one binding width from the cut edges. Turn and wrap the binding to the right side. Topstitch close to the foldline of the binding (see the illustration below).

DOUBLE-LAYER BINDING

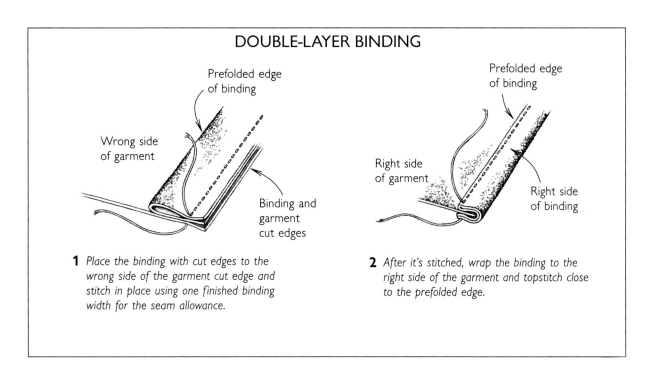

1 *Place the binding with cut edges to the wrong side of the garment cut edge and stitch in place using one finished binding width for the seam allowance.*

2 *After it's stitched, wrap the binding to the right side of the garment and topstitch close to the prefolded edge.*

ELASTIC

Elastic is a useful edge for cuffs and hems. It can be used in fleece and pile the same way it's used with other sportswear applications. To apply elastic, zigzag or serge it to the fabric while stretching it to the wrong side of the cut edge. Turn the elastic to the wrong side and straight-stitch or zigzag while stretching the fabric. Elastic threaded through a casing will work, but to prevent the elastic from rolling up during wear, run a stitching line or two through all layers. An alternative casing for elastic is a printed fleece border that is slightly wider than the elastic. It can be straight-stitched or zigzagged on the outside (or inside) of the garment.

Choose a sport-weight elastic that isn't too narrow and has a lot of spring to it. There are sport elastics available now that have vacant channels for topstitching through to prevent stretching out the elastic. However, I find it difficult to determine where the channels are in the bulk of the fleece.

The tricky part of doing an elastic edge is getting the right ratio of the length of elastic to the length of the fleece edge because the thickness of the fleece stretches out the elastic. On many elastic applications for less bulky fabric, the suggested length of elastic is 10% to 15% less than the body measurement. For example, if the waist measures 30 in., the elastic to be applied to the garment for the waist should measure 25½ in. to 27 in. With fleece, I usually take another 5% more off the length of the elastic. The finished results will depend on the thickness of the fabric, the strength and return of the elastic, and the number of stitching lines sewn through it.

To test the results, you should make a sample with premeasured pieces of fabric and elastic. For the sample, cut the elastic 8 in. long and the fabric 10 in. long. Stitch the cut ends of the elastic to the ends of the fleece to make it easier to get a precise measurement. Apply the elastic and then measure the results. This will tell you how much the elastic has grown in the stitching process and may help you calculate if you need to make your elastic shorter or longer for the application you've chosen.

RIBBING

You've probably seen many instructions for using ribbing, but there are a few things to note when using ribbing with fleece and pile. The weight and fiber content of the ribbing should be appropriate to the fleece. Nylon, acrylic, and other synthetics are available in ribbing and have strength and water resistance appropriate for using with fleece, but it can be difficult to find a good selection of color. The synthetic fabrics are especially nice if you can find a ribbing with a spandex blend.

The same problem of ratio applies to ribbing as it does to elastic. Each ribbing has a different return, and you want to be sure you don't have a body-hugging ribbing on the bottom of a loose jacket, or vice versa. Determine the fit of the ribbing to the body before attaching it to the garment by holding the folded ribbing around the body at the area where it will be on the garment and marking the desired length.

When attaching ribbing at the bottom of a jacket that has a separating zipper, use a piece of interfaced fleece or woven fabric to make a carrier at either end of the ribbing (see the illustrations on the facing page). This will produce a better result when stitching the zipper in place. The stretch of the ribbing will cause it to pull and buckle if it's stitched directly to the zipper tape.

ADDING CARRIERS TO RIBBING

1 *Cut a piece of stabilized fleece or woven fabric the same length as the width of the unfolded ribbing and as wide as desired (at least 3 in.). Interface the carrier to the fold. Stitch it to the end of the ribbing, right sides together. Turn the carrier to the right side and topstitch with seam allowances under the stitching line. Stitch one edge of the prepared ribbing to the bottom of the garment, stretching the ribbing as needed and keeping the carrier at a 1:1 ratio with the garment.*

2 *Stitch the separating zipper to the center front of the garment and the carrier, right sides together.*

3 *To enclose the zipper in the carrier edge, clip through the seam allowance at the fold of the carrier and then fold the carrier right sides together with the seam allowance of the unstitched edge turned down for easy finishing. Stitch through all layers at the edge of the carrier.*

4 *When the carrier is turned with the right side out, the zipper is ready to be topstitched for a sharp front edge. The remaining inside edge of the ribbing can be stitched to the bottom of the lining or topstitched in place in a single-layer garment.*

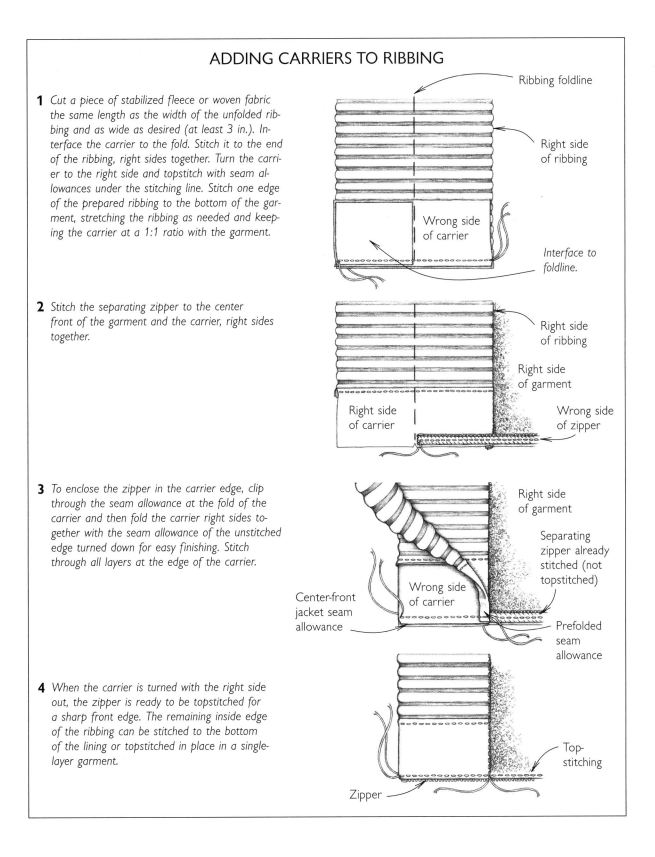

Ribbing foldline

Right side of ribbing

Wrong side of carrier

Interface to foldline.

Right side of ribbing

Right side of garment

Right side of carrier

Wrong side of zipper

Right side of garment

Separating zipper already stitched (not topstitched)

Center-front jacket seam allowance

Wrong side of carrier

Prefolded seam allowance

Top-stitching

Zipper

Stitch parallel rows from the cut edge to the ribbing line. Pivot and stitch from the ribbing line to the cut edge.

Zigzag the fleece cording to the edge. If there's rippling in the cut edge, flatten the work with your fingers or palm as you stitch.

To create a mock rib made from fleece, use a separate piece of fleece (crossgrain borders can work well) or make a ribbed edge from extra length cut on to the garment. Cut the garment pieces to the total length desired (including any blousing ease) plus an extra ½ in. Using chalk, a basted stitching line, or a wash-out marker, make a line at the top of the ribbing area.

Set the stitch length for the longest setting (not a basting stitch), and increase the upper tension of your machine to eight or nine. (There may be some variation for different machines, so as always make a test sample first.) Use a zigzag foot or a three-groove pintuck foot and a 4.0 stretch double needle, or the widest double needle available for your machine.

Starting at one end of the lower edge on the right side of the fabric, stitch parallel rows from the lower cut edge to the ribbing line (see the top photo at left). Backstitch at every starting and stopping point to secure stitching. I prefer to do this procedure in a continuous stitching line, lifting the presser foot and needle only far enough to change directions and release the tension of the thread as the fabric is pivoted under the presser foot. That way I don't have to clip the threads on each row.

The lower edge can be left as it is or finished with a same-color or contrasting-color edge of fleece cord. Cut a narrow crossgrain strip of fleece, stretch it firmly, and then zigzag it to the edge of the ribbing, with the cording flat but not pulled taut. If there is any rippling along the rib edge, use your palm to flatten the work as you stretch the fleece cording slightly while zigzagging the two together (see the bottom photo at left).

POCKETS

Pockets need to work with the aesthetic design of the garment, but the intended function has everything to do with the design. An active-wear jacket needs pockets that will work with the activity. For example, a ski jacket needs pockets that are work-able while wearing ski gloves and that are large enough to hold ski gloves, necessary safety equipment and food, or a hat or extra layer of warmth. And there must be enough pockets to store all of these items. In addition, ex-posed pockets need zippers and flaps.

A cycling jacket, on the other hand, benefits from less bulk at the front, so eliminat-ing the front pockets is an option. Pockets for carrying small items work well on the back of cycling jackets, with zippers to keep the contents from falling out. The fleece jacket at right that goes un-der a cycling jacket outer lay-er has a large zippered back pocket and side-seam pockets with microfleece backing to minimize bulk. The side-seam pockets are only meant for occasional use as hand-warmer pockets. The outer layer of the cycling jacket has no pockets on the front and a zippered pocket on the back. Each pocket should follow its

A large back pocket and smaller hand-warmer pockets are ideal for a fleece cycling jacket.

purpose in its size, location, shape, closure, and the size and shape of the flap.

In constructing a garment with one or more pockets, try to make the pockets before the garment is assembled (unless the pockets are in the seam) because after the main seams have been sewn it is difficult to maneuver the body of the garment while stitching the details of the pocket.

Patch pockets

Patch pockets are generally the most simple, but they can be very functional for certain purposes. By definition, a patch pocket is a separate piece of fabric that is sewn to the surface of another fabric (like a patch that covers a worn spot) and that has an opening to form a pocket. (See Jo's Haiku jacket on p. 38 for an example of patch pockets). For fleece, patch pockets can be topstitched on with a straight or zigzag stitch, stitched on with a trim, or bound with contrasting fabric and then stitched. If the pocket will be exposed to rain, use a flap over the top of the pocket to prevent it from collecting moisture. Most patterns have instructions for this type of pocket, so I won't go into specifics here.

In-seam pockets

Pockets that are sewn into the seam are quick and low profile. They work well as zippered pockets in a yoke seam. But keep in mind if you use a side-seam pocket as a hand-warmer on closer-fitting garments, it will throw off the line of the garment as the arms pull the garment forward. So use these pockets only in jackets and vests that have a loose-fitting design with extra ease in the shaping of the back.

Pocket bag or backing material should be made from lightweight fleece, mesh fabrics, or synthetic taffetas that are compatible with the washing method of the outer fabric.

In-seam pocket applications are easy to find in commercial patterns. To add a zipper to this type of pocket, mark the intended opening in the seam (see the illustration on the facing page). Stitch the seam, stopping and backtacking at either end of the opening. Open up the seam allowances and place the zipper's right side to the open seam allowance. Position the zipper tab at the desired location and pin it in place to the seam allowance only. With the fabric on the bed of the machine and the zipper tape under the presser foot, stitch the zipper in place, starting and stopping parallel to the ends of the pocket opening.

Keep the body of the garment out of the stitching line.

Cut a rectangular piece of fabric for the pocket bag a few inches wider than the zippered opening and twice as long as the desired finished-pocket depth. Center the short edges of the pocket bag to the wrong side of the zipper tape. Stitch through the seam allowance, zipper, and pocket bag just outside of the previous stitching line. Trim any excess outer fabric from the seam allowance. Topstitch along both sides of the zipper opening $\frac{3}{8}$ in. from the edge on the right side of the garment, keeping the pocket bag out of the stitching area.

Fold the pocket bag to the direction it will lie when the garment is worn. Pin the remaining cut edges of the pocket bag, stitch the long edges of the pocket bag from the fold to the edges at the zipper, keeping the body of the garment away from the stitching line (a zipper foot may be necessary to stitch past the ends of the zipper). If the corner of the pocket bag hangs below the bottom of the jacket when it's worn, add a curved shape to the bottom of the pocket bag, then cut off the excess seam allowance. Use a bar tack or topstitch the ends of the pocket with the bag in the correct position.

ADDING A ZIPPER TO AN IN-SEAM POCKET

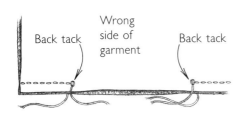

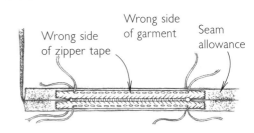

1 *Stitch the seam, leaving an opening for the pocket by back-tacking at either end of the pocket area.*

2 *Stitch the zipper tape to the seam allowance of the pocket opening, right sides together, keeping the garment free of the stitching line. Start and stop stitching parallel to the zipper stop (or the desired beginning and end of the opening).*

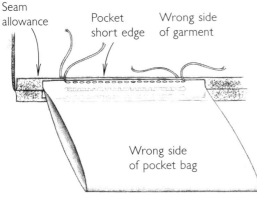

3 *Center the right side of the pocket bag along the short edge of the pocket and the wrong side of the zipper tape. Stitch through the seam-allowance layers only. Start and stop stitching parallel to the zipper stop.*

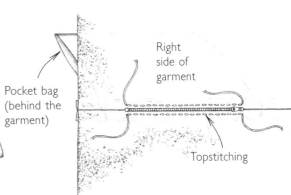

4 *From the right side of the garment, topstitch through the seam allowances ⅜ in. from the edge of the zipper, keeping the pocket bag free of the stitching line. Start and stop stitching parallel to the zipper stops.*

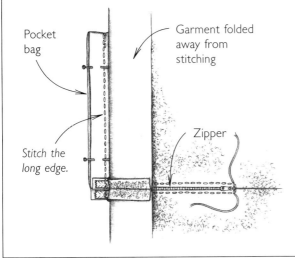

5 *Position the pocket as it will lie in the finished garment (usually to the front). Pin it and stitch the long edges of the pocket bag, keeping the outside of the garment free of the stitching area.*

IN-FABRIC ZIPPERED POCKET WITH A POCKET BAG

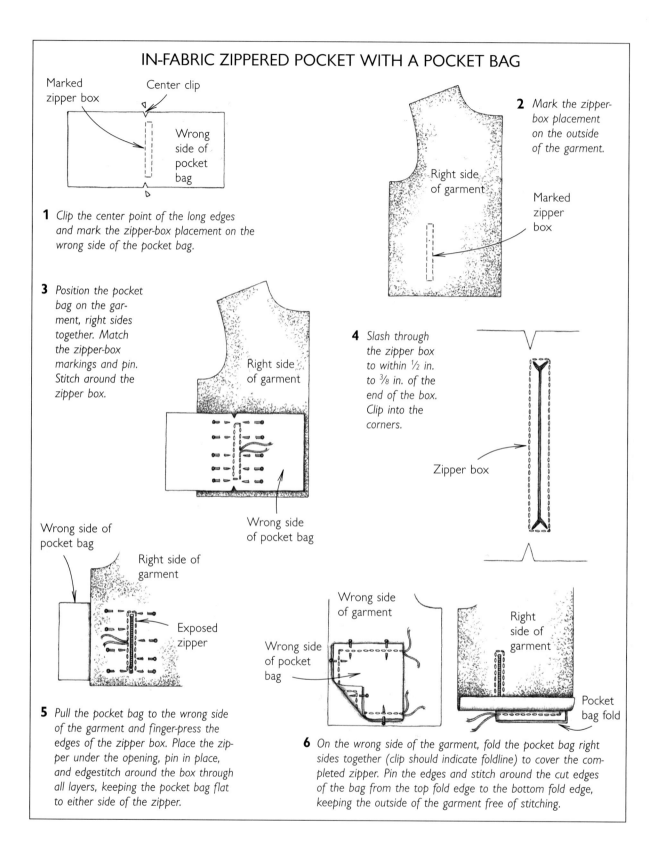

Marked zipper box

Center clip

Wrong side of pocket bag

1 *Clip the center point of the long edges and mark the zipper-box placement on the wrong side of the pocket bag.*

2 *Mark the zipper-box placement on the outside of the garment.*

Right side of garment

Marked zipper box

3 *Position the pocket bag on the garment, right sides together. Match the zipper-box markings and pin. Stitch around the zipper box.*

Right side of garment

Wrong side of pocket bag

4 *Slash through the zipper box to within ½ in. to ⅜ in. of the end of the box. Clip into the corners.*

Zipper box

Wrong side of pocket bag

Right side of garment

Exposed zipper

5 *Pull the pocket bag to the wrong side of the garment and finger-press the edges of the zipper box. Place the zipper under the opening, pin in place, and edgestitch around the box through all layers, keeping the pocket bag flat to either side of the zipper.*

Wrong side of garment

Wrong side of pocket bag

Right side of garment

Pocket bag fold

6 *On the wrong side of the garment, fold the pocket bag right sides together (clip should indicate foldline) to cover the completed zipper. Pin the edges and stitch around the cut edges of the bag from the top fold edge to the bottom fold edge, keeping the outside of the garment free of stitching.*

Chapter Four

In-fabric zippered pockets

For activewear I prefer to use a zippered pocket that can be located anywhere in the fabric. There are many different methods for installing this type of pocket, including a modification of the in-seam pocket technique.

With a pocket bag One option is to attach a pocket bag to the garment then attach the zipper (see the illustration on the facing page). First, cut a pocket bag a few inches wider than the desired zipper opening and twice as long as the desired pocket-bag depth plus two seam allowances and 1 in. Clip the center point of the two long edges. Draw a zipper box the length and width of the desired zipper opening on one side of the centerline with chalk or a wash-out marker. Remember to reverse the pocket-bag markings for right and left pockets. Mark the right side of the garment with the pocket placement.

Match the pocket bag to the markings on the garment, right sides together. Pin in place and stitch around the zipper box using a medium-length stitch. Slash through the zipper box and clip into the corners. Trim the fleece seam allowance. Finger-press the pocket bag to the back of the garment. Place the zipper under the zipper-box opening and pin it in place. Edgestitch around the zipper. Fold the pocket bag, right sides together, then stitch around its cut edges, keeping the body of the garment free of the stitching line.

A second option is to stitch the zipper box directly into the body of the garment and stitch the zipper in after the box is slashed open (see the photos below and on pp. 84-

Stitch the zipper-box shape into the outer fabric.

Slash open the zipper box and cut diagonally to the corners.

Place the zipper facedown along the cut edge.

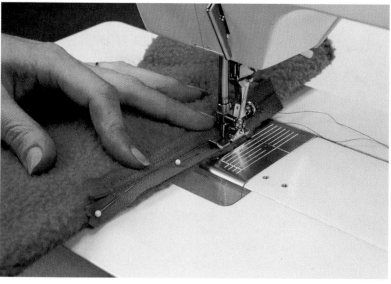

Stitch with the zipper tape on top and the fabric on the bed of the machine.

85). To begin, stitch the zipper-box shape in place (see the top photo on p. 83), then slash the zipper box open and clip into the corners (see the bottom photo on p. 83). Place the zipper face down along the cut edge (see the top photo at left). Stitch the long edge of one side of the box from one corner to the other, with the zipper on top and the fabric on the bed of the machine. Secure the ends of the stitching lines with a back tack. The clip inside the zipper box should end right at the ends of the stitching line.

Fold the zipper through to the wrong side and align the loose edge of the zipper with the other side of the zipper box, right sides together. Stitch in the same manner as before, with the zipper tape on top and the fabric on the bed of the machine (see the bottom photo at left). Fold the fabric across the end of the zipper box to expose the triangular shape against the end of the zipper. Stitch across the triangle to secure it (see the photo on the facing page). Edgestitch around the zipper opening.

The pocket bag may now be stitched in the same manner as the in-seam method or cut as two separate pieces and sewn to the seam allowance of the zipper tape, or you can make a pocket back.

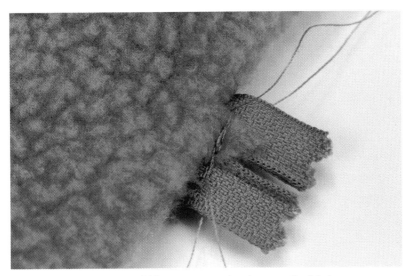

Stitch across the triangle of fabric to secure the zipper to the fabric.

With a pocket back If you want a pocket with a lot of capacity but don't want a floppy pocket bag (such as in an unlined jacket), you can use the technique described above to apply a pocket backing that is stitched to the back of the outer fabric.

Modify the opening by making a facing for the zipper a few inches wider than the zipper box (see With a pocket bag on pp. 83-84), or be creative with the facing shape and size. To attach the facing, stitch it to the wrong side of the garment, slash it open, clip into the corners, turn it, and topstitch it to the right side of the garment (see the illustration at right). Stitch the zipper under the box in the same manner. If you don't want to use a facing, simply stitch a zipper

ZIPPER OPENING WITH AN EXPOSED FACING

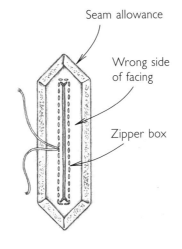

Seam allowance

Wrong side of facing

Zipper box

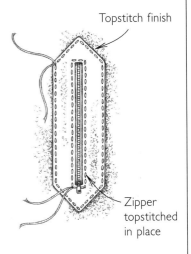

Topstitch finish

Zipper topstitched in place

1 *Cut the facing shape and press the outer-edge seam allowances to the wrong side of the facing. Place the right side of the facing to the wrong side of the garment, stitch the zipper-box opening, slash through the box, and clip into the corners. Trim the excess fleece seam allowance.*

2 *Turn the exposed facing to the right side and press (or finger-press) the edge of the zipper box. Place the zipper under the box, pin, and topstitch in place. Pin and stitch the outer edge of the facing in place.*

Sewing Tips & Techniques

TOPSTITCHING A POCKET BACK

Large-capacity pocket back

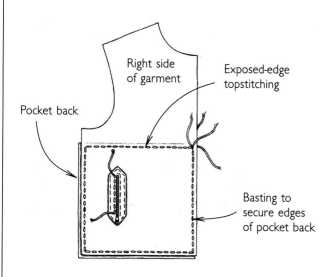

Right side of garment

Exposed-edge topstitching

Pocket back

Basting to secure edges of pocket back

A large-capacity pocket back is made in the same shape as the lower portion of the garment and then stitched in place around the cut edges before the garment is assembled. The exposed upper edge is topstitched in place. The outside edge of the zipper is topstitched through all layers to keep them from moving independently.

Hand-warmer pocket back

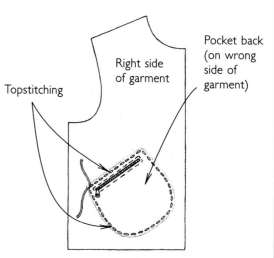

Pocket back (on wrong side of garment)

Right side of garment

Topstitching

This pocket back is shaped for a hand-warmer pocket and stitched to the back of the garment through all layers.

box, insert the zipper (see the photos on p. 83-85), and then topstitch around the opening.

You can make a pocket back in any shape. It may be the same shape as the pattern piece it is sewn to or a slight variation where topstitching connects the backing to the outer fabric at the top and the other edges are basted to the outer fabric at the seamline before assembly (see the left illustration above).

Although the pocket back may be any shape, you should avoid sharp angles in the bottom of the pocket because they catch small items and will drive you crazy when you try to get things out of them. I've found that a long semicircular pocket back with a zipper placed at an angle is one of the most comfortable applications of the pocket-back technique (see the right illustration above).

To keep the outer fabric from moving independently of the pocket back, topstitch through all layers on the stitching line at the top edge of the pocket. Straight-stitch or zigzag the back to the outer fabric. After the pocket back has been applied and all edges are secured, it can be treated as one piece while assembling the garment.

Flaps

It's easy to minimize the value of flaps on pockets, but they are actually very important, especially in an outer-shell garment. They prevent rain from collecting in your

---

MAKING A SHAPED POCKET FLAP

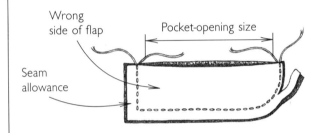

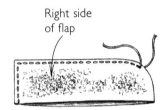

1 Make two identical pocket-flap shapes slightly longer than the opening. Interface the flap pieces, then place them right sides together. Stitch around the outside edge, and grade seam allowances.

2 Turn the flap to the right side and topstitch around the outer edge.

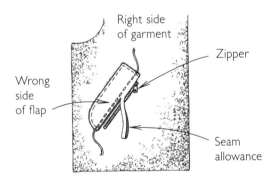

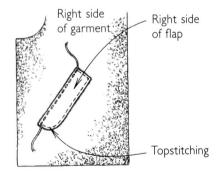

3 Place the right side of the flap together with the right side of the garment, with the cut edge of the flap parallel to and centered with the upper edge of the pocket opening (and the zipper). Stitch through all layers and grade seam allowances.

4 Fold the flap across the pocket opening (and the zipper) and topstitch to secure. To make the pocket more water resistant, topstitch the upper short edge of the flap as well.

---

pocket, and that means a lot when it's time to warm up your hands. Flaps can also minimize the effect of the pocket on the design line. And they can enhance the design of the garment when they're made in unusual shapes or contrasting colors.

When designing the flap pattern yourself, compare the finished flap size and shape to the space it is meant to fit by placing the flap pattern over the pocket area on the larger pattern piece. Do this before putting the zipper in because you may find the pocket will work better if it's put in at a slightly different angle. Drawcords, side seams, hems, and other design elements create boundaries that need to be considered when creating a flap pattern.

If you want a snap or button closing on a fleece flap, you'll need to stabilize the closure with a compatible woven fabric for the top or bottom fabric.

The basic method for making a flap is simple (see the illustration on p. 87). Cut two pieces of fabric the same shape. They should be slightly longer than the pocket plus seam allowances and wide enough to cover the pocket opening by a few inches plus seam allowances. Stabilize the flap with a nonfusible interfacing or a compatible woven

fabric. With the right sides together, stitch around the outside edges of the flap, trim the seam allowances, turn the flap to the right side, and topstitch around the outer edge. Place the remaining cut edge of the flap parallel to the upper edge of the pocket opening (above the zipper), right sides together. Stitch, trim the seam allowance, fold the flap over the stitching line, and topstitch. Backstitch at the beginning and end of the stitching to secure the ends.

You may want to mirror the binding techniques used on other edges of your fleece and pile garment when making flaps. In that case, trim the seam allowances from those edges and bind with the same binding technique.

CLOSURES

Closures are critical in the end use of a technical garment. They need to work without fail in extreme conditions. With more casual wear, it is only a headache or a disappointment when the closures don't function well.

With a selection of closures in your "toolbox," you can find the most appropriate type for each garment and expand on the possibilities with your own flair and style.

Snaps

A greater selection than ever before is available to the home sewer when it comes to snaps. The best sources are generally through mail-order companies that specialize in outerwear fabrics, snaps, and/or other notions (see Resources on p. 131).

Snaps come in two different types: post back and prong back. Heavier applications (parka, multilayers) should use a heavy-duty post-back snap. It is important, though, to reinforce the fabric that the post penetrates if the fabric is knit. Otherwise the fabric will stretch away from the post when in use, and the snap may pop out. Reinforcement can be made with a backing layer of densely woven compatible fabric used as a facing, with sewn-in interfacing, with a topstitched wide binding, or with individual appliqués under the snap area. Some of the new low-temperature fusible interfacings may be beneficial between two layers with a snap. The hole for the snap (which can be cut like a tiny cross or poked with a leather punch) should be made slightly smaller than the post so that the fabric has to stretch tightly around it.

The prong-back snap works with lighter-weight fabrics or single-layer garments. When installing the snaps, follow the directions on the package and make sure the prongs penetrate the snap securely. Prong snaps have difficulty penetrating dense synthetic fabrics, so test them on a sample before trying them on the garment.

Buttons and buttonholes

There are some considerations when making button closures that are particular to fleece because of its knit structure and its thickness. As far as buttons go, choose ones that are large enough to easily manipulate through fleece (shank buttons are a good option) and that are compatible with the care of the fleece.

The buttonholes have some other considerations. The fabric needs to be reinforced to prevent rippling. When the garment edge has a facing, a low-temperature nonfusible interfacing may be inserted to stabilize the knit, or if the fabric is flat enough, a fusible interfacing may be used. Another option for stabilizing the edge is to use a coordinating woven fabric as a wide binding or facing, and then to stitch buttonholes in this edge.

If the edge will be bound, a quick fold of a woven fabric aligned with the edge before binding will reinforce the but-

tonhole area easily. Or use the same idea on the outside of the garment to create a contrasting placket. The cardigan on p. 11 has an inside placket made from woven nylon; it is interfaced, then the edge is seared with a hot tool before it's edgestitched to the back of the fleece (see the illustration below).

I think one of the most useful tips I can give you about making a machine-stitched buttonhole in fleece is to stitch it with the wrong side up and the right side of

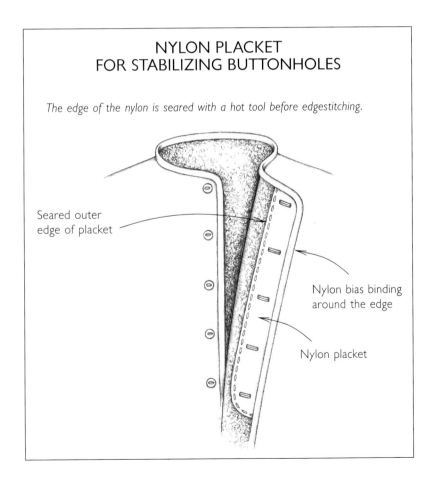

NYLON PLACKET FOR STABILIZING BUTTONHOLES

The edge of the nylon is seared with a hot tool before edgestitching.

Seared outer edge of placket

Nylon bias binding around the edge

Nylon placket

FLEECE-CORD BUTTONHOLES

Cut buttonhole openings the desired length for the button by two widths of premade fleece cord. Holding the cord taut (but not stretched) under the work, zigzag it to the long inside edges of the cut buttonholes on both sides of the opening. Bar-tack the ends of the buttonhole opening through all layers. Trim the excess cord from the back side of the work.

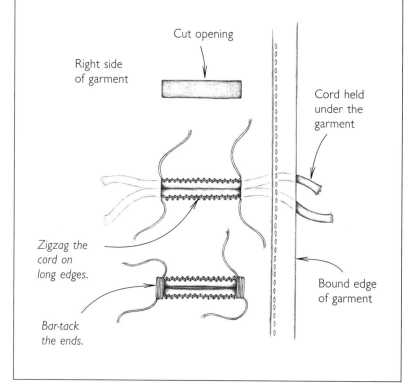

Cut opening

Right side
of garment

Cord held
under the
garment

Zigzag the
cord on
long edges.

Bound edge
of garment

Bar-tack
the ends.

tension slightly before stitching the buttonhole on the wrong side.

Fleece cording can be used to finish the inside edge of a large buttonhole. Cut a buttonhole shape in the fleece garment that allows for two widths of the cording, then zigzag the cording to both inside long edges of the cut opening (see the illustration at left). Bar-tack both ends through all layers to finish and trim excess cord ends.

Button loops and ties

Button loops and ties are easily made from crossgrain-cut fleece cording. Cut the strips of fleece narrow enough that the cut edges roll to create cording when stretched out. Braid long sections of cord that can then be divided into short loop sections for stitching into the garment. Use a short straight stitch across the braid to divide the loop into sections, then cut the sections apart. The individual sections can be sewn into the front-edge seam or binding to make the button loop, or the ends can be bar-tacked together in the desired location. For a textural effect, you may wish to leave curly tails at the end of the loop. (You can see button loops on the pile coat on p. 15.)

Braided ties for closures can be made in the same

the fleece on the bed of the machine. Because the machine naturally wants to pull the bobbin thread up, some machines make a tension adjustment to draw the top thread down into the fabric (on a Bernina, the bobbin thread is threaded through the hook to give increased tension). Instead of using these counteractive measures, increase the upper thread manner as braided button loops. Then they are attached to the garment with multiple rows of short topstitching or by bar-tacking in place, as in the hat on p. 119.

Hook-and-loop tape

Usually called by the brand name Velcro, hook-and-loop tape is a closure choice that many people prefer because it's easy to apply. However, the rough texture of the hook tape can be very irritating, so don't place it in a location where it will be in contact with the skin. If you are using a tab at the neck or cuff, place the softer loop side on the surface facing the skin.

There are some distinct disadvantages to using hook-and-loop tape that are important to keep in mind. Multiple front and cuff hook-and-loop closures in the same garment tend to get caught together when the garment isn't closed. And the hook tape picks up fibers from sweaters, fleece, and pile and loses its effectiveness if it isn't cleaned out. When using strips that are more than a few inches long, it's hard to make the opposite sides line up because as one end of the strip is being attached, the other end is attaching itself to somewhere it's not supposed to be. Longer strips also detract from the natural drape of the fabric of the garment and look like stiff patches on the front flap of your garment.

Hook-and-loop tape can be very useful for an adjustable cuff, but I've tried using it on front flaps of parkas and ended up ripping it out and installing snaps because it was so annoying to have it catch on everything.

DRAWCORD AND CASING

With fleece and pile, a drawcord may not pull easily through a casing made of self-fabric. A synthetic woven-fabric casing makes the drawcord more effective. To make the casing, rip or cut cross-grain strips the desired width and length of the casing plus two seam allowances in each direction.

Before stitching the casing to the garment, locate where the cord will come through the garment and apply an opening—an eyelet, grommet, or buttonhole—to the stabilized area. (If the opening is going on fleece or pile fabric only, reinforce the area with a patch of woven synthetic fabric sewn to the back of the garment.) Mark the upper and lower placement lines on the wrong side of the garment.

To attach the casing, turn under the casing seam allowances at the short ends, and stitch, with the right side of the casing to the wrong side of the garment, at the upper placement line. Fold the casing over the stitching line, turn under the remaining seam allowance, and edgestitch the remaining edge to the lower placement line (see the illustration on p. 92). If the cord has a separate casing, like a hem casing, make a narrow rolled hem at both ends before stitching the casing to the garment.

For a more flexible drawcord, cut a section of 3⁄8-in. swim elastic one-third the length of the flat casing. Stitch two one-third lengths of drawcord securely to either end of the elastic so that the resulting piece measures the same as the casing. Be sure the drawcord will fit through the casing opening, or you may have to leave a section of the casing open to get the cording in place.

Cordlocks, also called toggles, keep the cord from being drawn back into the casing. They come in barrels, balls, rectangles, and discs. To add one to a cord, squeeze the cordlock, thread the cord through the cordlock's hole, and release the cordlock. Knot the drawcord end to prevent pulling the cordlock off when adjusting it.

DRAWCORD AND CASING

Casing for a drawcord at the waist can be made from a woven, water-repellent fabric and stitched to the wrong side of the garment. A buttonhole or grommet can channel the cord through to the right side of the garment. A separate casing at the hem of the garment can have the short ends stitched with a rolled hem before being stitched to the garment.

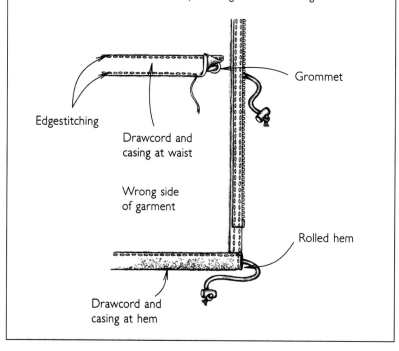

Edgestitching

Drawcord and casing at waist

Grommet

Wrong side of garment

Rolled hem

Drawcord and casing at hem

ZIPPERS

I'm always surprised that people find sport zippers so daunting. I have found them easier to install than most dress zippers! There are many features to consider when selecting sport zippers, such as style, material, and size. Availability will be a determining factor in your choice. Local availability may be quite limited, though, so try some of the sources listed in Resources (p. 131). If you are lucky enough to find a source that has manufacturers' excesses, you may find some terrific zippers.

Most patterns designed for fleece that include a sport zipper have instructions for sewing it in, but here are some general instructions for zipper application and some special finishes—more tools for your "toolbox."

Separating zippers

Some people are confused by the term separating zipper—after all, don't all zippers separate? A separating zipper is a zipper that comes completely apart at the bottom and is used primarily at the center front of a jacket or vest. Separating zippers have variations, such as the one-way zipper (one pull tab), the two-way zipper (two pull tabs—one pulls up from the bottom when the zipper is closed), and the reversible zipper (the pull tabs are accessible to both sides of the zipper).

To install a separating zipper (see the photos on pp. 96-97), the key is to make sure that both sides of the garment to be joined by the zipper align perfectly before, during, and after the zipper is installed. For an example, we'll use a center-front zipper. When the two front pieces are placed together, the

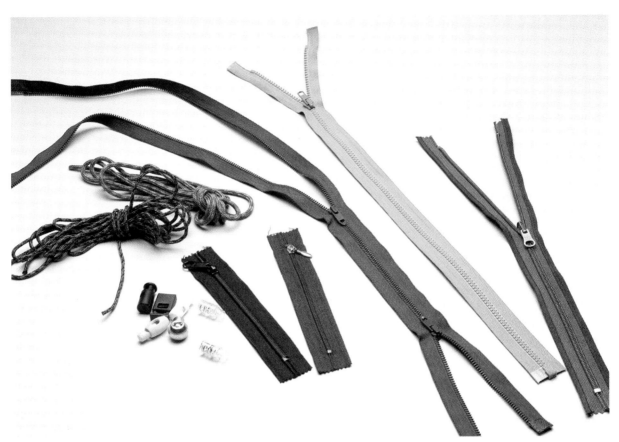

Zippers, cording, and cordlocks come in a variety of weights and styles.

top of the collar, neck seam, yoke, pocket, hem, and any other symmetrical details should be matching before you pin the zipper in place. If they aren't and you slightly stretch the fleece fabric (even unintentionally) to make it fit, the zipper will distort the finished garment. If the matching points line up, pin one side of the zipper in place, right sides together (see the photo on p. 96).

Baste the zipper in place with the zipper tape on top and the fleece fabric on the bed of the machine (see the top photo on p. 97). Fold the zipper back and use a wash-out marker or chalk to mark across the zipper tape perpendicular to points that need to be matched on the remaining zipper edge. Pin the remaining front edge to the zipper, matching the zipper-tape marks to their matching points on the fabric. Baste the zipper in place with the same technique used on the first side of the zipper, then check the right side to see the results. If you are not binding the edge of the zipper

Making a Zip-Apart Parka

An easy way to create zip-apart garments is to use the same pattern for both the inner and outer garments, making changes to the separate patterns so the finished garments will hang together easily. Side seams for the inner garment can be closer to the body, and armscyes can be shorter than for the outer garment. Shoulder slope and neck shape should stay relatively the same for both garments, though you may wish to adjust the neck slightly higher in the front on the inner garment. Keep any change to the center front in mind when you stitch the connecting zippers in place.

You have to prepare two sets of zippers that will be sewn into the garments after they are close to completion. (The closing for the outer garment is unrelated to the zippers for attaching the inner garment, so develop that separately.) You need two separating zippers that are identical, although they don't have to be the

---

ZIPPER ASSEMBLY OF A ZIP-APART COMBINATION

After the inner garment is constructed, zip on the corresponding outer-garment half zippers to each side, which will be sewn to the inner edge of the outer garment. The attaching zipper can be pinned to the inside edge of the outer garment. Check to make sure the zipper lies flat before stitching it in place.

A protective flap made from straight-grain woven fabric can be added to cover the inner zipper of the outer garment. It should extend over the top and bottom of the zipper by ½ in. or more and be wide enough to cover the exposed zipper when the two garments are zipped together.

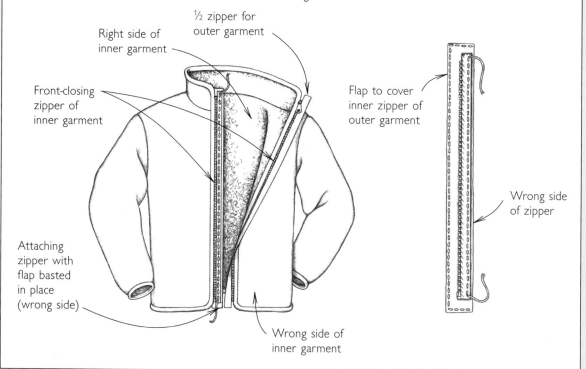

Right side of inner garment

½ zipper for outer garment

Front-closing zipper of inner garment

Flap to cover inner zipper of outer garment

Wrong side of zipper

Attaching zipper with flap basted in place (wrong side)

Wrong side of inner garment

---

same color. They should be tested before installation to ensure that each will zip to the corresponding part of the other zipper.

After the front-closing zipper for the inner garment is installed, zip the corresponding zipper parts (those that will be sewn to the inside of the outer garment) to each side of the installed zipper. These are the attaching zippers (see the left illustration on the facing page). A simple, straight-grain folded flap or single-layer fleece flap may be basted to the outside edge of the zipper that will be sewn to the outer garment to cover the exposed zipper teeth (see the right illustration on the facing page). Try on both layers and pin the outside edges of the zipper in place, making adjustments if the layers don't hang right. The back-neck and shoulder seams should lie together.

The outside edge of the attaching zipper can be stitched to a facing edge or to the edge of the outer-layer zipper, button placket, or any other center-front seam allowance.

To help keep the inside garment (or lining) from separating when you take the garment off, attach hook-and-loop tape on single-face fleece tabs, then stitch them in strategic locations on the inside of the outer garment (see the illustration below). The hook is abrasive, so don't leave it exposed to the skin. A soft loop cord should be stitched in the same locations on the inner garment so that the tabs can be attached through the loops to secure the garments together.

HOOK-AND-LOOP TABS AND CORD LOOPS

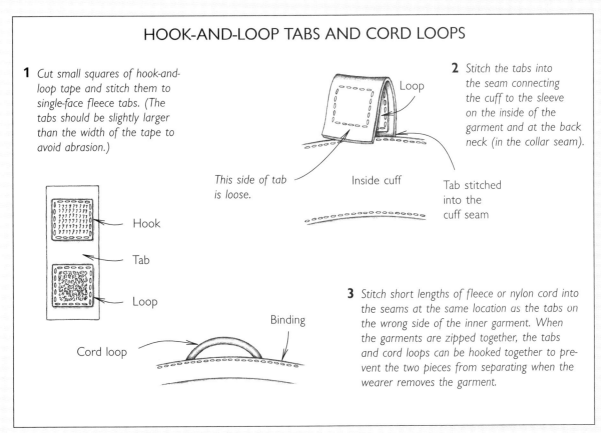

1 Cut small squares of hook-and-loop tape and stitch them to single-face fleece tabs. (The tabs should be slightly larger than the width of the tape to avoid abrasion.)

Hook

Tab

Loop

Cord loop

Binding

Loop

This side of tab is loose.

Inside cuff

Tab stitched into the cuff seam

2 Stitch the tabs into the seam connecting the cuff to the sleeve on the inside of the garment and at the back neck (in the collar seam).

3 Stitch short lengths of fleece or nylon cord into the seams at the same location as the tabs on the wrong side of the inner garment. When the garments are zipped together, the tabs and cord loops can be hooked together to prevent the two pieces from separating when the wearer removes the garment.

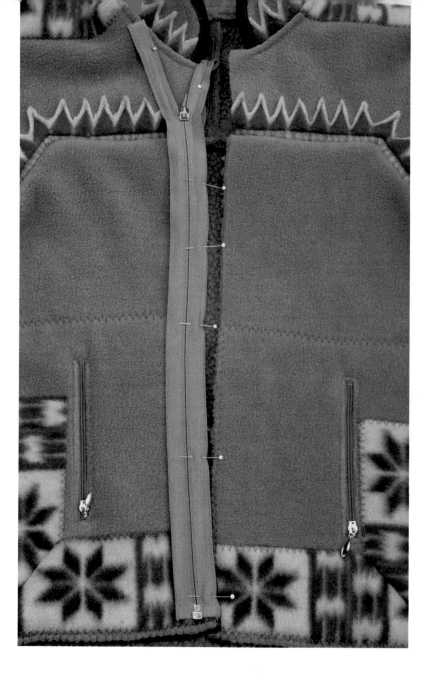

tape (as described on pp. 98 and 99), trim the seam allowance before topstitching the zipper from the right side. When topstitching, keep the fabric pulled gently away from the zipper to avoid the fleece getting twisted or puckering along the zipper (see the bottom photo on the facing page).

Once the zipper is pinned, baste it in place.

Gently pull the fabric away when top-stitching next to the zipper.

Shortening a Separating Zipper

You may have to settle for a zipper that isn't exactly what you wanted because often the ideal length is not available. To shorten a separating zipper, fold out the excess zipper at the top and stitch the zipper in place. Try to align the stitching so the needle will go between the zipper teeth. If you don't stitch very slowly (you may want to turn the flywheel by hand), it's easy to break the needle. Trim off the excess zipper only after the length you need is stitched in. The teeth on the excess are at an angle to create a stop for the zipper pull. A zipper shortened this way benefits from binding on the edges to hide the cut-off ends (see Binding the edge of a zipper below) or from a small piece of grosgrain ribbon wrapped around the area.

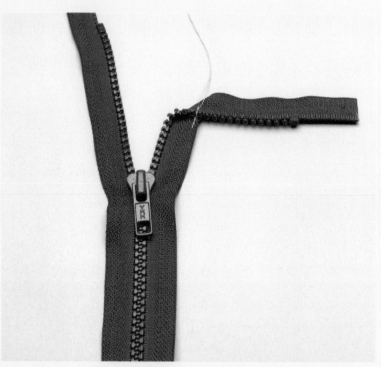

Don't cut off the excess from a separating zipper before stitching because it's too easy to zip off the pull if you do.

Binding the edge of a zipper

A nice way to finish a zipper in an unlined garment with exposed zipper tape is to bind the edge of the zipper with a bias-cut woven or microfleece fabric using one of the procedures for binding shown in the illustrations on pp. 70 and 71. Finish the ends of the binding with the same technique shown in the top illustration on p. 67. The binding can be sewn on before or after the zipper is stitched to the garment (see the photos on the facing page).

Here are some more tips on binding zipper tape for easier stitching on multiple layers:
- When binding the zipper tape, treat the back of the zipper as the right side so the finished side will show after the zipper is installed.
- Use a zigzag foot with the needle position adjusted closest to the zipper teeth instead of a zipper foot; it keeps the work flatter and the presser foot more level.
- Don't cut the fleece seam allowance away until the first stitching line of the binding has been made. It will prevent the presser foot from tipping to one side.
- Use a grosgrain ribbon as an option for binding the zipper tape. To attach it, use the binding method for synthetic suede on pp. 72-73.

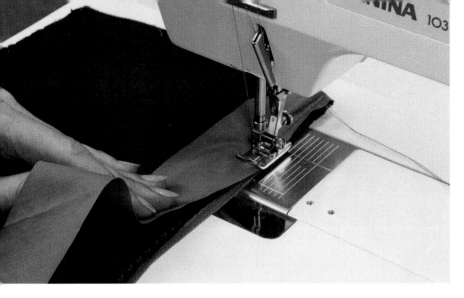

Bind the inside of the zipper tape by stitching on the inside first (left) and finishing on the wrong side of the zipper tape (below).

Installing a nonseparating zipper

A nonseparating zipper can be installed in a seam or in the middle of the fabric. When there is no seam, the procedure is much the same as for the pocket zipper.

Stitch a box where the zipper will be, slash open the box, and clip into the corners. Place the zipper and fabric right sides together, with the zipper extending below the triangular cut at the bottom of the zipper box (see the illustration on p. 100). Stitch outside the zipper stop from corner to corner (with the bottom of the zipper box under the stitching), and reinforce with a backstitch. Fold the zipper through the box and align it with an inside cut edge, right sides together. Stitch from corner to end with the zipper on top and the fleece on the bed of the ma-

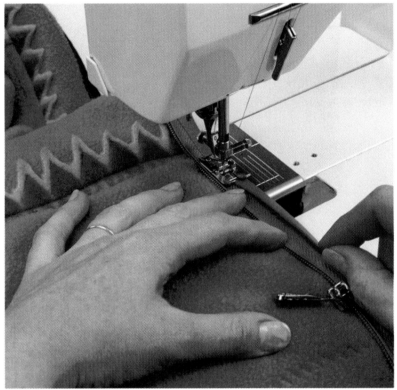

chine. Repeat for the other edge. Topstitch, or finish with a binding.

You can install a leg zipper on warm-up pants in a similar manner (see the illustration on p. 101). After the

pants' side seam has been stitched and topstitched, baste across the end of the stitching where the top of the zipper will be, or stitch the whole box shape. The ends of this short stitching line will

INSERTING A ZIPPER WHEN THERE IS NO SEAM

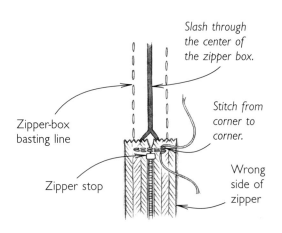

Slash through the center of the zipper box.

Zipper-box basting line

Stitch from corner to corner.

Zipper stop

Wrong side of zipper

1 *Stitch a zipper box where the zipper will be located. Slash through the box to ½ in. above the bottom, and clip into the corners. Place the right side of the zipper to the right side of the garment below the zipper box. With the zipper stop centered just below the zipper box, stitch from one corner to the other corner through the zipper.*

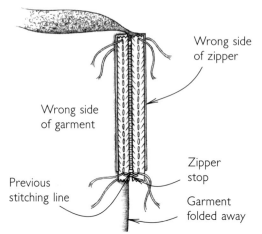

Wrong side of zipper

Wrong side of garment

Previous stitching line

Zipper stop

Garment folded away

2 *Fold the zipper through the zipper box to the wrong side of the garment. Position the zipper so that the zipper tape lines up parallel to the cut edge of the zipper opening. Stitch in place, starting or ending at one end of the previous stitching line.*

be the corners and the beginning of the stitching line for the zipper sides. Clip into the corners at an angle. Continue as for any zipper, but remember the zipper should extend above the triangular cut on the pant-leg application. The zipper stitching lines will be just outside of the seamline (or on the zipper-box stitching if you have stitched one).

Here are some additional tips on zipper installations:
- Use a narrow fleece border zigzagged to the back of the zipper edge for a quick edge finish (see the photo on p. 32).

- Apply the zipper to the garment edge, wrong sides together, and use a border or trim to finish the zipper edge on the right side of the garment.

LINING

Fleece and pile make excellent liners and are simple to put in. Follow the instructions on your pattern, but keep these things in mind:
- The lining pattern should be smaller than the outer-shell pattern, so trim the lining pattern at the side and underarm seams if necessary.

- Seam allowances should be topstitched and trimmed where possible to keep bulk from showing on the outer layer.

- Fleece sleeve linings may not allow easy on and off because they can catch on another garment's sleeve, so try using a satiny fabric for all sleeve lining, or layer it with a thin fleece secured with quilting lines. (The upper back might benefit from this technique as well.)

LEG ZIPPERS

1 *Stitch the side seam to the top of the zipper placement and reinforce with a backstitch. Clip through the seam allowance at an angle down toward the end of the stitching. Stitch half the zipper box on each side of the opening with the top of the box just outside the end of the side seam.*

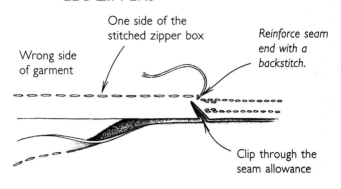

One side of the stitched zipper box

Wrong side of garment

Reinforce seam end with a backstitch.

Clip through the seam allowance

2 *Turn the seam allowances to the right side and pull the clipped ends out from the work. Place the right side of the zipper together with the right side of the garment, with the zipper stop just above the zipper box. Stitch across the zipper below the zipper stop, with the stitching starting and ending in each corner of the zipper box. From the wrong side, clip to the corners of the zipper box through the seam allowance.*

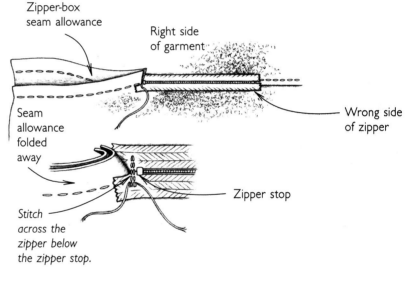

Zipper-box seam allowance

Right side of garment

Seam allowance folded away

Wrong side of zipper

Stitch across the zipper below the zipper stop.

Zipper stop

3 *Fold the zipper to the wrong side. Align the zipper tape parallel to the seam allowance edge so that it can be stitched right over the zipper-box stitching line. Pin and stitch in place. Repeat for the other side of the zipper.*

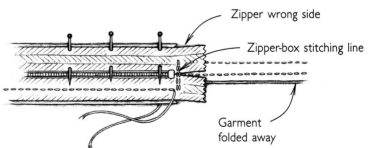

Zipper wrong side

Zipper-box stitching line

Garment folded away

5

WRAPPING UP

We've already looked at many construction techniques for fleece in jackets, pants, and vests. These techniques and expressive details are also applicable to a multitude of other items such as blankets, slippers, and hats. This chapter will give you a starting point for other uses of fleece, but don't hesitate to experiment. You never know where your own ideas will lead you!

BLANKETS

Many fleece projects are easy, but few are easier than a blanket. A 2-yd. cut of fleece as it comes from the bolt will function quite nicely as a blanket. (You may wish to trim off the selvages first, however.) Choose from a variety of fabric weights, finishes, and patterns.

Fleece blankets are very practical and so easy to make that they can simply be cut to the blanket size desired and quickly finished with a variety of edges—a bound edge with woven bias binding, straight-grain binding, spandex binding, a coordinating border print, blanket stitch (see Decorative stitches on p. 65), or fringe—or left with no edge finish. Whatever edge you choose, you can jazz up the blanket with some unique appliqués or decorative stitching to create a new type of handmade heirloom.

Sarah's sweater dress can be worn casually with leggings for an autumn stroll or dressed up for dinner at a ski resort.

Stitching Mitered Corners in Binding

It's easier to make stitched mitered corners in a blanket binding by first marking the width of the finished binding to the right of the machine needle on the bed of the machine with removable tape. (The example shown below is based on a 1½-in. finished binding with a ½-in. seam allowance.) Align one edge of the blanket wrong side up along the tape marking. Place the binding right side down with only the seam allowance to the right side of needle (see step **1** below). Stitch, keeping the binding and fleece in these positions. When approaching a corner, stop and secure stitching one binding width (1½ in.) from the cut edge and backstitch. Raise the presser foot and clip the binding seam allowance to the end of the stitching, being careful not to cut through the thread. Fold out two binding widths (3 in.), clip through the seam allowance to mark it, and pin in place (see step **2** below). Stitch to the corner clips, pivot, and reposition the fabric so that the binding continues from the clips and stitching continues from the previous stopping point at a 90° angle. Repeat this process at each corner.

1 *Place the binding right side down with only the seam allowance to the right side of the needle. Stitch to one binding width from the perpendicular cut edge, backstitch, and drop the needle. Clip through the binding seam allowance to the end of stitching.*

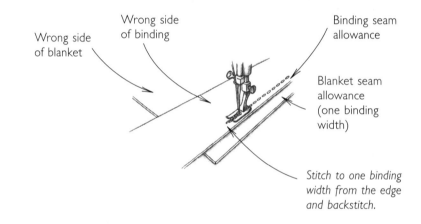

Wrong side of blanket

Wrong side of binding

Binding seam allowance

Blanket seam allowance (one binding width)

Stitch to one binding width from the edge and backstitch.

2 *Fold out two binding widths, clip through the seam allowance to mark, and pin to the end of the stitching line. Continue stitching, pivoting at the corner clips (keep excess binding away from stitching line).*

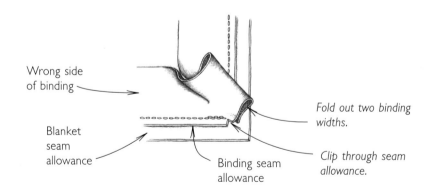

Wrong side of binding

Blanket seam allowance

Binding seam allowance

Fold out two binding widths.

Clip through seam allowance.

Make seamed miters before stitching the remaining edge of the binding. To do this, fold the binding flat across its width with the corner clips matching, then pin and clip through the binding seam allowance at the loose edge parallel to the corner clips. Stitch from the end of the clips at the outer seamline to the center foldline. At the fold, pivot and continue stitching to the seamline directly across

from the starting point. (Stitching lines will be at a 45° angle to binding for square corners. See step **3** below.) Clip the seam allowance of the binding at the fold to the center (the pivot point). Finger-press the seam allowances of the stitched miter open and wrap the binding around the blanket edge. Fold under the binding seam allowances of the remaining edge, pin them in place with the

folded edge overlapping the previous stitching line so that the new stitching line will be off of the binding on the other side. Topstitch or zigzag to finish (see step **4** below).

3 *To make seamed miters, stitch the first pass as shown in step 2, folding out the binding at the corners. Before stitching the remaining edge, fold the binding across the width at the corner clips. Pin and clip through the seam allowance parallel to the corner clips. Stitch from the end of the clips at the outer seamline to the center foldline, pivot, and continue stitching to the seamline clips of the first stitching line. Clip the center fold to the center pivot point.*

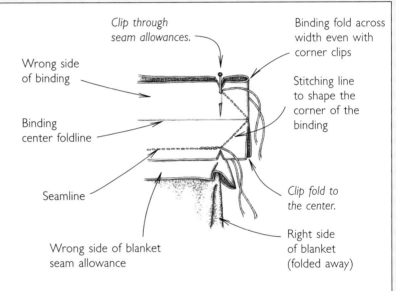

Clip through seam allowances.

Wrong side of binding

Binding center foldline

Seamline

Wrong side of blanket seam allowance

Binding fold across width even with corner clips

Stitching line to shape the corner of the binding

Clip fold to the center.

Right side of blanket (folded away)

4 *To finish, turn under the cut edges and topstitch (left) or zigzag (right).*

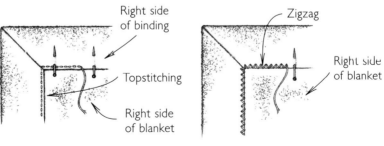

Right side of binding

Topstitching

Right side of blanket

Zigzag

Right side of blanket

Blanket binding

When making a bias blanket binding, you have many choices of fabric types for the binding, from lightweight to mid-weight woven cottons (sateen is nice) to polyesters in taffeta and satin. Generally, any fabric that will wash and dry under the same conditions as the fleece fabric and isn't stiff when used in a double layer will work as a binding. Remember to pre-wash and dry the binding fabric before cutting. This will help prevent the shrinkage of natural fibers and the excess-color bleeding of nylon fabrics. (Avoid using intense neon or fluorescent colors of nylon that may continue to bleed after many washings.)

To construct a blanket with a bias binding, measure the circumference of the blanket piece. Then cut woven binding strips on the true bias twice the width of the desired binding plus two seam allowances. For example, for a 1½-in.-wide finished binding with ½-in. seam allowances, the total width would be 4 in. Join the bias strips, right sides together, and stitch at a 90° angle (see p. 68 for more information on cutting bias strips).

Fleece border edge

Blankets may be finished nicely with a distinctive fleece border. Cut and join the lengths of the border using a butted or lapped seam with a zigzag (see Butted and lapped

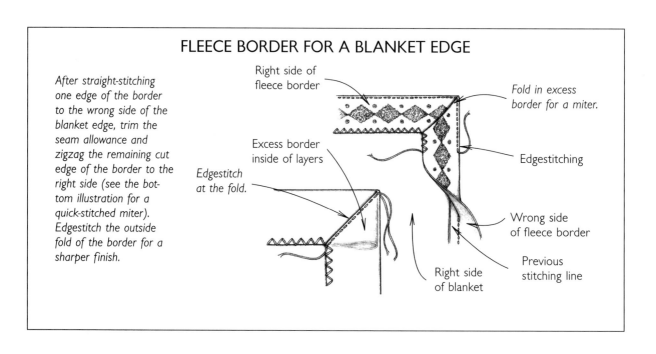

FLEECE BORDER FOR A BLANKET EDGE

After straight-stitching one edge of the border to the wrong side of the blanket edge, trim the seam allowance and zigzag the remaining cut edge of the border to the right side (see the bottom illustration for a quick-stitched miter). Edgestitch the outside fold of the border for a sharper finish.

Right side of fleece border

Fold in excess border for a miter.

Excess border inside of layers

Edgestitching

Edgestitch at the fold.

Wrong side of fleece border

Previous stitching line

Right side of blanket

Design Details with Borders

Borders can be used as appliqués, edges, trims, and bindings. They are a colorful way to liven up a blanket, or even a jacket or skirt. And with the large variety of fabrics to choose from, you're sure to find something you like.

Borders are cut from printed fabrics. They are most useful when printed on the crossgrain of the fabric because the extra stretch gives the fabric flexibility for trimming around curves and for maintaining the ease of fit when trimming on fleece and pile. If a stable trim were to be used, the garment wouldn't stretch in that area that had the trim.

One fabric may have several possibilities for cutting lines, so look at the fabric carefully to determine which line would be the most interesting. Sometimes a straight edge is the easiest and most practical use of a border design, but others may have curves and angles, which can produce unusual effects.

To use a single layer of border on the edge of a garment, place the cut border on the partially constructed garment and pin it in place as you would any other straight trim. Slightly stretching the border as you pin will help keep it from buckling while you stitch. Fold out the miters at the corners (see the illustration on the facing page and the photo below) and pay attention to whether the print matches well on the miter.

To curve borders, match the outermost edges of the border flat with the curved main fabric (or slightly stretch the border fabric on a shallow curve) and pin in place. Shape the inside edge of the border by easing excess at the curve or stretching the ground fabric on a shallow curve. Narrow borders will curve easily without having to ease in excess on the inside of a curve.

When making arrangements of borders on shoulders and yoke areas, prearrange and pin before stitching in the same manner as for a straight border, using mitering, curved edges, and free-motion stitching to produce the desired effect.

Fleece borders are easy to work with. When sewing miters, fold excess trim inside at the corners.

seams on pp. 58-59) until the length measures the circumference of the blanket plus a few inches. You can use the border as you would bias binding except instead of stitching it with seam allowances, topstitch a cut edge with the wrong side of the border to the right side of the fleece, folding out the miters as you go. Straight-stitch the first edge to the wrong side, then zigzag the remaining edge to the right side so that stitching will overlap the binding edge on both sides. Edgestitch the outside fold of the border for a sharper edge.

For a different edge that's flat with a more distinctly defined edge, stitch two borders together along one edge. This can now be used as a binding by stitching with the wrong side to the blanket edge (see the illustration below).

Decorative/embroidered trim edge

Another way to finish the edges is a purchased decorative trim. There is a wide variety of embroidered trims that would quickly finish a fleece blanket. Take care to preshrink trim using the same wash/dry method that will be

used for the blanket. Begin by edgestitching the trim to the wrong side of the fleece edge. Fold the entire width of the trim to the right side and topstitch the loose edge in place, folding the miters to the inside (see the illustration on p. 106). Miters can be folded in then stitched down to keep them from gapping.

Fringe

Fringed edges are a quick and easy way to finish a blanket without sewing. For the fringe to lie flat, it should be cut perpendicular to the width on a knitted fleece or pile (paral-

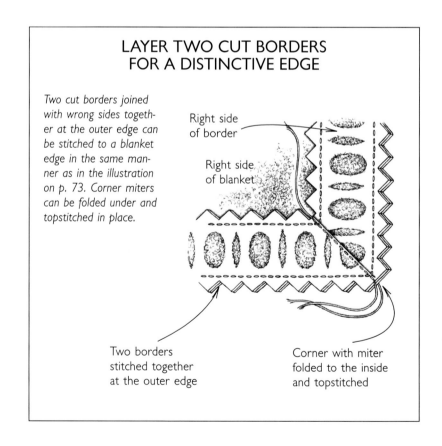

LAYER TWO CUT BORDERS FOR A DISTINCTIVE EDGE

Two cut borders joined with wrong sides together at the outer edge can be stitched to a blanket edge in the same manner as in the illustration on p. 73. Corner miters can be folded under and topstitched in place.

Right side of border

Right side of blanket

Two borders stitched together at the outer edge

Corner with miter folded to the inside and topstitched

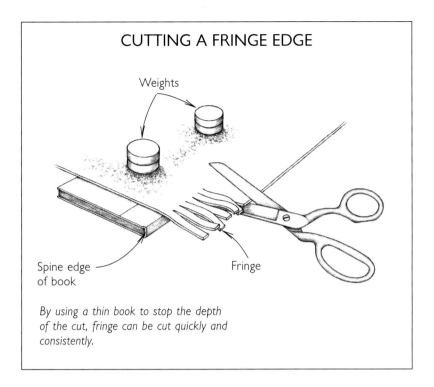

CUTTING A FRINGE EDGE

Weights

Spine edge of book

Fringe

By using a thin book to stop the depth of the cut, fringe can be cut quickly and consistently.

lel to the grain). If the fringe is cut along the length of the fabric, it will curl when it is pulled, which is normal during use. Mark the depth of the fringe along the width of the fabric using chalk or wash-out marker, then mark the cut edge equal distances for the desired width of the fringe. Using sharp scissors, clip the length of fringe in one cut. To make sure the fringe length is equal for each cut, lay the fleece on a table with the spine of a thin book under the depth line, and place fabric weights on top of the fleece (see the illustration above). When you cut, the bottom part of the scissors will stop at the same spot on each cut.

Baby blankets

Baby blankets are truly appreciated when made from fleece. A 45-in. by 60-in. piece will make a terrific wrap for a newborn. Babies like to run their fingers along a smooth satin edge (my daughter used to rub her lips with the satin edge), so choose a binding that has that type of sensory appeal *and* is durable–you never know how much love and abuse that blanket will get!

BUNTINGS

A bunting is like a blanket that is cut more to the shape of the body. For an adult, it's a simple bag with a zipper for wearing while knitting, reading, or watching TV. Some versions have loose arms attached at the upper body. For a baby, there are patterns for buntings that make the process of bundling them up much easier (see Resources on p. 131). For example, a feature such as cut-on mitts that fold back so that baby's hands can be uncovered is especially important if the baby needs thumb access. Other useful features are a zip-open

CONVERTING A BUNTING FOR CAR-SEAT USE

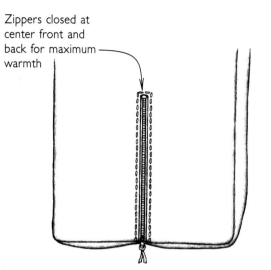

Zippers closed at center front and back for maximum warmth

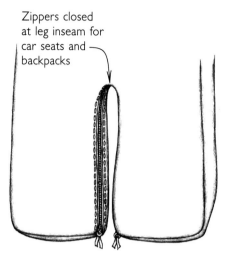

Zippers closed at leg inseam for car seats and backpacks

With short separating zippers installed at the lower center-front line and center-back line, a bunting can be zipped so that the lower portion is one large bag (left). Or, when each zipper is separated and zipped to the other corresponding zipper part, the bunting can have individual legs to fit more easily into a car seat or a baby backpack (right).

front for easy in and out and diaper changes and double-separating zippers at the lower edge that convert the bag into legs, making the bunting easier to use in a car seat or a baby backpack (see the illustration above).

It's easy to forget while out walking with a baby that, though the person pushing the stroller (or carrying the backpack) is getting a nice aerobic workout, the baby is relatively immobile and experiences a lot of heat loss when not adequately protected. So use a heavier fleece for the bunting, one with a wind barrier, or use a double layer (fleece or woven nylon) on the front and back of the upper body. Try to prevent abrasive edges near the baby's skin, especially the face. Use flaps and tabs around zippers, and keep hook-and-loop tape away from the skin. Toggles for drawstrings should be on the outside, away from the face.

ROBES

Most major pattern companies have robe patterns that work well with fleece. With so many variations of style and types of fleece to choose from, it may be difficult to decide what might work the best. Narrow it down by determining the main use for the garment. Heavier-weight fleece is wonderful on cold mornings in February, but after a hot bath it would be too warm. Though fleece wicks, the amount of heat and vapor your body produces after a bath is much greater than normal, so a lightweight fleece with a light cotton lin-er or a mid-weight double-face fleece would be more appropriate for after a bath.

If you use a traditional construction method for a wrapped robe, most patterns provide a collar-facing pattern piece, hemmed patch pockets, a tie made from a double lay-er, and possibly a sleeve-hem facing. Multiple layers of fleece can make these areas look too thick, especially when you use heavier weights of fleece, so use the tech-niques in the sidebar on p. 55 for flat-seaming meth-ods to minimize the bulk and to help you choose an inter-facing, if you so desire.

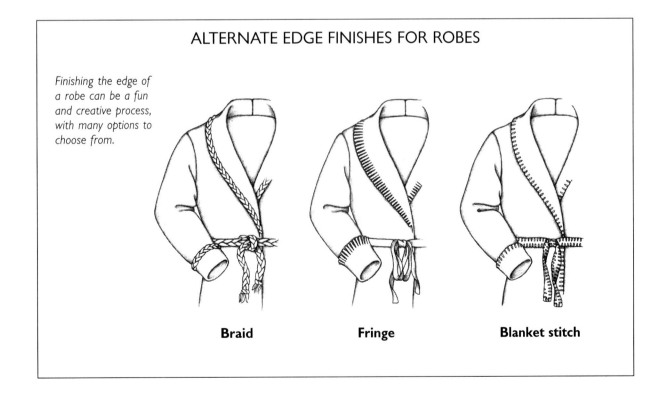

ALTERNATE EDGE FINISHES FOR ROBES

Finishing the edge of a robe can be a fun and creative process, with many options to choose from.

Braid   **Fringe**   **Blanket stitch**

You may want to trim down this look by using binding or serged decorative thread to flatten the edges and to create a more streamlined effect. Before cutting out, trim the seam allowances from the collar, front edges, and around the patch-pocket edges. Trim the hem allowance from the lower edge and the top of the pocket, and cut one layer of the tie without seam allowances. When constructing the robe, use binding techniques, serging, or a blanket stitch on these edges to finish (see the illustration on p. 111 for decorative finishes). Zip-front robes and kimonos can also be made using some of these same techniques.

Measure the pieces of your flat pattern at the hips and bust. Compare those measurements to your own, adding in ease. Adjust the pattern accordingly, folding out or adding as necessary. With all of these pattern types, there is a tendency to have too much ease built in because they are designed for cotton terry, which has no stretch, or for a lighter-weight fabric, like kimonos. (See the sidebar at left for more on ease in looser-fitting garments.)

Kimonos in a lighter-weight fleece are an interesting translation of an old favorite. For the neck banding, tie, and cuffs, use a coordinating cotton woven where it's useful to have a more stable fabric. Use fleece fabric to interface the cotton band so that the thickness of the attached pieces will be similar to the thickness of the fleece. Pin and baste the fleece interfacing piece to the wrong side of the woven piece close to the seamline, with the fleece on the bed of the machine. Trim excess fleece to the basting line, then treat it as one piece. After turning to the right side, topstitch the edges to finish.

Determining Ease on Looser-Fitting Garments

A loose-fitting garment like a robe or oversized coat doesn't need the precise fit of a tailored jacket, but a general-ease measurement appropriate to the body and the design of the garment is helpful for pattern comparisons. To determine general ease, wrap a tape measure around the widest part of the body. Hold one end of the tape measure between your thumb and forefinger and place the loose end between your forefinger and middle finger. Slide the loose end of the tape measure, making it larger or smaller until you get an idea of how much extra room, or ease, you want in the garment.

This way of measuring produces very general results and is best used for loose-fitting robes and oversized coats. (You may need two tape measures and help from a partner to measure for larger designs.) Use this same method to measure for the cuff width on a robe. Cuffs are often too long for my taste. Since I like to cook breakfast in mine, I don't like the cuff hanging in the pancake mix.

PAJAMAS

Pajamas should be made in lighter-weight fleece because heavier weights may be too warm. It's easy to underestimate fleece's capacity for heat retention. When sleeping under covers, less air moves around the body, resulting in less breathability. I've found a 100-weight microfleece usually works well. Heavier weights for small children and babies is appropriate because they have a tendency to kick off their blankets during sleep and can lose precious body heat quickly.

Because of the extra bulk of fleece and its natural stretch, choose a pajama pattern that is close to the body rather than a looser style, which is used for lighter cotton or cotton-blend pajamas.

Footed pajamas can be made with gripper fabric for the outer sole of the feet. The fabric comes in small sheets in the notions department or by the yard in some stores. Gripper liquid latex that can be brushed on is also available where rug-making supplies are sold.

Using a flatlock on the major seams or another flat-seaming technique (see Seams on p. 56) you can produce very comfortable pajamas. By eliminating the seam allowance, you minimize abrasion next to the skin, and during those precious golden hours in bed, where we spend more time than anywhere else, the less agitation the better!

SLIPPERS AND SOCKS

Slippers and socks made from fleece are very popular. Soft and comfortable during most of the year (not too hot or cold), they wick away sweat to minimize smelly feet (though with some people, nothing helps!).

There are some advantages to making slippers and socks over purchasing them. For example, purchased slippers are often too wide, so the foot slides around inside. When you make your own, you can adjust the size of the pattern so that the slippers aren't too loose. Most of the adjustment will be in the width because of fleece's stretch in the crossgrain. For slippers and socks, choose the pattern size closest to the length of your foot by placing your foot on the pattern (give yourself an extra ¾ in. in length for ease). Check the width of your foot next to the pattern. You may want to draw a new outside edge on the pattern using the edge of your foot as a guide. This is where you can take out a lot of width.

Measure around the new pattern piece. Adjust the length of the upper pieces of the pattern to accommodate the new measurement. Take the extra length out evenly, distributing it from all pieces by folding out length and keeping any shaping intact. You may have to redraw the ankle opening. Because it takes such a small amount of fabric, make a sample and do some fine-tuning. The final slipper or sock will go together much faster.

Another option when making slippers and socks is to build in an arch. For those of us who have lost ours in years past and use artificial ones in our shoes, an arch greatly improves the comfort of slippers. The technique for making arches is like making a shoulder pad for your foot (see the illustration on p. 114). Cut arc-shaped pieces from extra fleece in two to three sizes using an arch support from your own shoe to determine what sizes you need. There is some guesswork here, and you may have some trial and error to get the right shapes, so make samples until the profile of the inner edge of the arch looks similar to the original.

To make the arch, zigzag the smallest piece on top of the mid-size piece. Place that piece on top of the large

ADDING A SOFT ARCH TO SLIPPERS OR SOCKS

1 *Match the inside edge of the smallest arch piece to the mid-size arch piece and zigzag.*

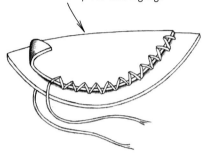

2 *Match the mid-size arch piece and the large arch piece in the same manner as the previous step and zigzag the outer edge.*

Stitch this edge to the instep.

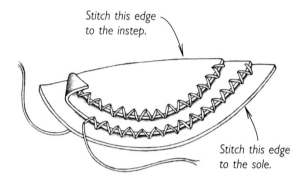

Stitch this edge to the sole.

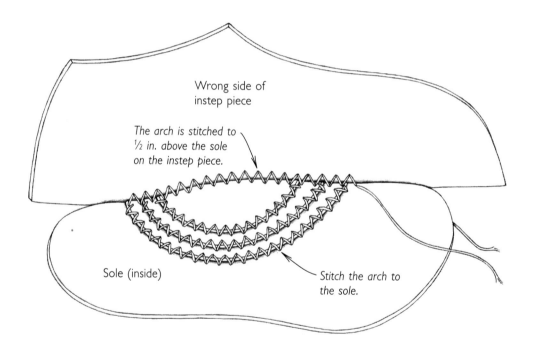

Wrong side of instep piece

The arch is stitched to ½ in. above the sole on the instep piece.

Sole (inside)

Stitch the arch to the sole.

3 *Match the inside edge of the large arch piece to the appropriate area of the sole piece and zigzag around the outside edge of the large arch piece. Match the instep slipper or sock piece and stitch the connecting seam at the arch area. Fold the instep piece against the arch, pin in place, and zigzag across the top so that the center of the arch is ½ in. or more above the sole piece.*

piece and zigzag around the mid-size one. Place the largest piece in the arch area of the slipper or sock, using a shoe to locate the correct position, then zigzag around it. If possible, when constructing the slipper or sock, stitch the inside edge of the arch to the inside of the upper part of the slipper or sock about ½ in. from the sole at the highest point.

Finish slippers with nylon or cotton/spandex ribbing at the ankle, or make the opening higher on the ankle and finish with spandex binding (see pp. 68-69). Like footed pajamas, slipper bottoms can be finished with gripper fabric or liquid gripper latex to prevent slipping. Cut gripper fabric with the same pattern as the sole. Baste the liner and gripper layers together and treat as one piece (use tissue paper over the gripper layer if it's difficult to stitch). Using leather or suede for a gripping surface on the sole is very common; however, it doesn't grip as well as the commercial gripping products. Don't use the gripper products on the soles of socks that are meant for use in shoes; it's too difficult to get your shoe on properly.

In the Northwest, where Birkenstocks have been the uniform of the casual class for years, fleece socks have been received enthusiastically. Fleece socks are similar to slippers and are often used that way, but if you make socks that are closer to the foot, they can be worn with a roomy shoe or boot. If possible, select a pattern that has an arced seam across the top of the foot at the front of the ankle. Otherwise you can cut out some of the bulk and seam it with a flatlock or lapped seam (see the illustration below).

For both socks and slippers, use a flatlock seam if possible because it can be stitched from the outside with both layers flat and will open

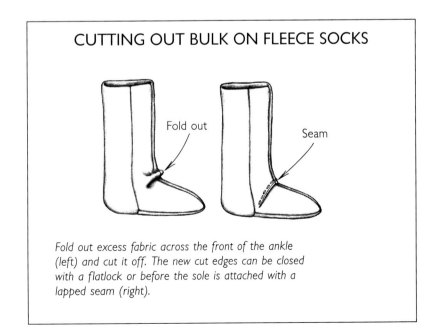

CUTTING OUT BULK ON FLEECE SOCKS

Fold out excess fabric across the front of the ankle (left) and cut it off. The new cut edges can be closed with a flatlock or before the sole is attached with a lapped seam (right).

flat to leave no seam allowances. A lapped seam–using a zigzag, cover stitch, or double needle–or a butted seam can be used, but it may be more difficult to stitch around the toe and heel area as the sock takes shape. These techniques produce a flat seam that has little bulk from seam allowances, which is much more desirable in a close-fitting sock or slipper. Seam allowances around the toe area are almost as annoying as getting your toe stuck in a hole in your sock.

HATS

I could write a whole book just about hats. Fleece is a great fabric for creating functional headgear and for crafting "sculpture for your head!" Its textural characteristics, colors, and slight stretch make it an ideal fabric for imaginative, adventurous "head trips."

"Boardheads" on the slopes of many western peaks brought fleece into the world of grunge, flying down slopes with stocking hats 6 ft. long, jester hats with 6 tails in 8 colors, and hats that looked like tie-dyed dreadlocks. It didn't take long for the fun of wild hats to shift to two-legged skiers and then into the mainstream.

When making hats, use binding and flat-seam techniques as much as possible. Most, if not all, of the cap-type patterns available on the market use a facing of fleece around the shaped crown next to the face, which makes a thick edge of four layers (counting seam allowances). You may prefer to use some of the binding techniques that we've shown in Chapter 4 and bind the edge of a shaped crown piece with nylon/spandex. A single or double layer of fleece bound with spandex conforms to the shape of the head, and the binding draws the edge next to the face to eliminate drafts. Cut the crown pieces across the width of the fabric to utilize the cross stretch.

Hat brims are seen many ways: floppy, soft, stiff, wide, narrow, turned up, turned down, and turned up and down. Your pattern will determine a lot about the shape, but you can use the fleece to affect the character of the brim. Two layers of fleece with a symmetrically stitched design around the brim can create a stiffer effect without interfacing, but remember the more thread that is stitched into a fabric that isn't stabilized, the more the fabric grows. Nonfusible interfacing may be stitched into a brim for more stiffness, or you

may wish to try a fusible knit interfacing on the jersey side of single-face fleece.

For a flat, stiff brim, try using a fusible bond product (sold by the yard or in sheets) between two layers of single-face fleece. Cut the bonding sheet slightly smaller than the shape of the brim inside the stitching line. Don't stitch through it unless you're sure of its characteristics; some weights of fusible bond will gum up your needle.

I am including two hat patterns in this section: an adult hat that I call the Brimmed Beret and a child's hat that I call the Tripoint. The adult hat can be manipulated in many ways. The brim can be worn up or down, with or without a tied-on band or trim, pinned or not. The child's hat has the advantages of a contoured crown with shaped earflaps, a nylon/spandex bound edge for better fit around the face, and endless options for embellishing with borders, trims, or stitched effects. This hat is especially popular for babies and small children.

Brimmed Beret
This hat requires:
- ½ yd. of mid-weight fleece
- 1 yd. of 1½-in.-wide precut nylon/spandex binding
- 21⅜ in. of soft elastic

BRIMMED BERET PATTERN

Scale: 1 square = 1 in.

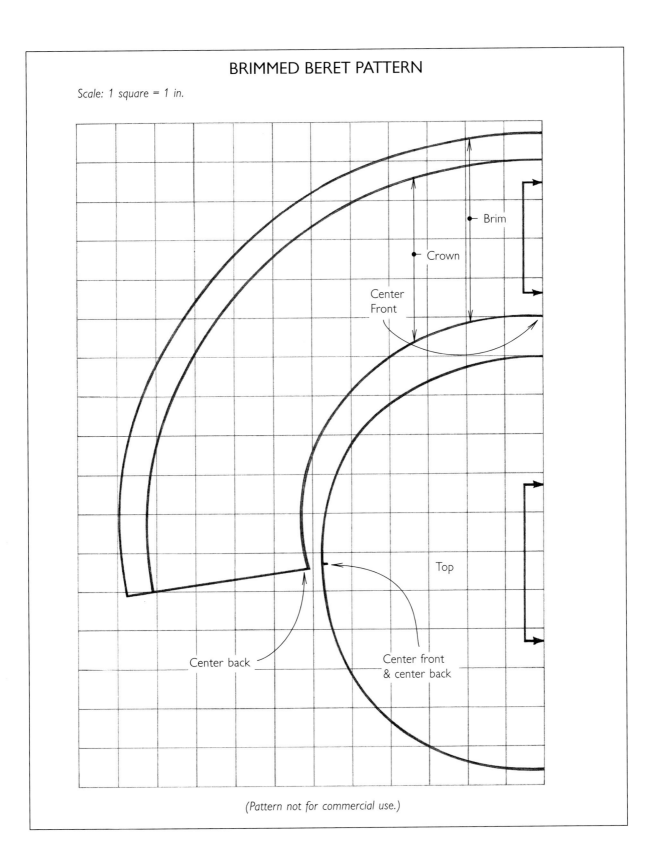

Brim

Crown

Center
Front

Top

Center back

Center front
& center back

(Pattern not for commercial use.)

MAKING THE BRIMMED BERET

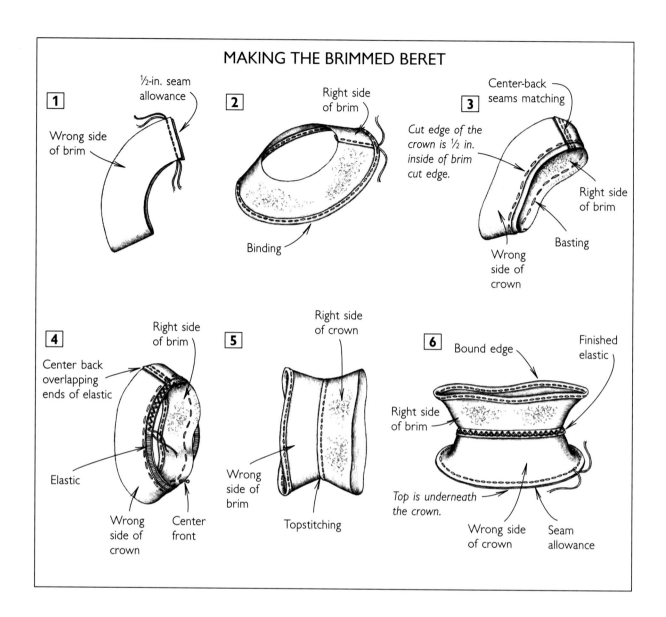

1 ½-in. seam allowance

Wrong side of brim

2 Right side of brim

Binding

3 Center-back seams matching

Cut edge of the crown is ½ in. inside of brim cut edge.

Right side of brim

Basting

Wrong side of crown

4 Right side of brim

Center back overlapping ends of elastic

Elastic

Wrong side of crown

Center front

5 Right side of crown

Wrong side of brim

Topstitching

6 Bound edge

Finished elastic

Right side of brim

Top is underneath the crown.

Wrong side of crown

Seam allowance

Transfer the pattern to a 1-in. grid (see the pattern on p. 117). The pattern pieces for the brim and crown are the same except for the width (the brim is ½ in. wider). Mark center front and back on all pieces.

With the right sides together, stitch the center-back seam (the short straight edges) of the brim using a ½-in. seam allowance (see step **1** above). Use a false flat-fell seam (see Topstitched seam on p. 56) or trim off the seam allowance and flatlock. (If using a flatlock seam, put the wrong sides together.) Repeat for the center-back seam of the crown. Bind the edge of the brim with spandex binding without stretching as you sew (see step **2** on the facing page).

Place the crown inside the brim with the right side of the crown to the wrong side of the brim. Pin at the inside edge of the center front and center back with the crown edge ½ in. inside the brim edge. Working with the wrong sides facing out, baste just inside the edge of the crown (see step **3** on the facing page).

Divide the elastic in half and mark it. Pin the mark on the elastic to the center front of the inside edge of the brim. Overlap the elastic at the center back and pin both ends. Beginning at the center back, zigzag the elastic to the brim edge using a large stitch and stretching the elastic to fit evenly between the pins (see step **4** on the facing page). Open the two layers. Working from the right side of the crown with the elastic edge turned under, topstitch through all layers with a straight or zigzag stitch ⅜ in. from the seam while stretching the elastic (see step **5** on the facing page).

Turn the crown wrong side out. Place the top and the crown right sides together, matching the center front and center back. Stitch with a ½-in. seam allowance and trim to ⅛ in. (see step **6** on

This Tripoint hat, which coordinates with Maddie's vest on p. 32, has colorful braids and tassels made from fleece cording. (Photo by Scott Phillips.)

the facing page), or trim off the seam allowance and flatlock with wrong sides together. Turn the hat to the right side. (See the photo on p. 53 for the finished hat.)

Tripoint hat

To fit a child 2 years old to preteen, this hat requires:
- ½ yd. of lightweight to mid-weight fleece
- border of choice, approximately 2 in. to 3 in. wide
- 2 in. to 3 in. of fleece in coordinating colors for tassels and braids

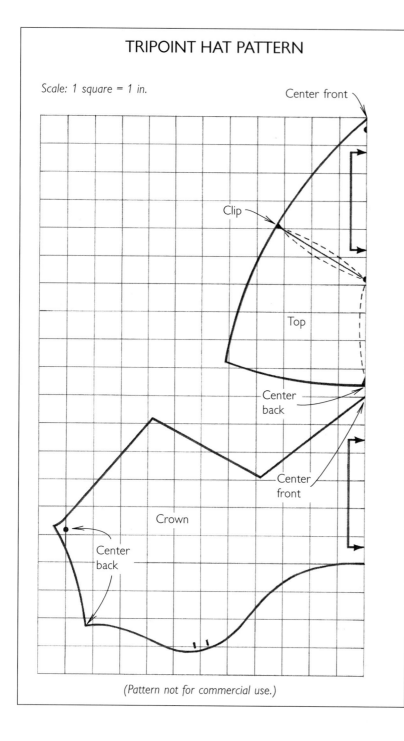

TRIPOINT HAT PATTERN

Scale: 1 square = 1 in.

Center front

Clip

Top

Center
back

Center
front

Crown

Center
back

(Pattern not for commercial use.)

- 30 in. of 1½-in.-wide nylon spandex binding
- 3 lightweight bells (if desired)

Transfer the pattern to a 1-in. grid (see the pattern at left). On the top piece, mark the center of the edgestitched spokes on the wrong side and clip notches at the end of each spoke (located at the midpoint of each side). Mark which notch is the center back (see step **1** on p. 122). This is important because the grain will be altered if the center back is rotated.

Fold the top with the right sides together so that the center-back notch and the center mark of the spokes is aligned. Edgestitch a narrow (⅛-in.) dart from the center-back notch to the center mark using a straight stitch, and secure the ends of the stitching line with a backstitch. Drop the needle at the center (see step **2** on p. 122). Raise the presser foot and reposition the fabric so that the fold extending from the needle ends at another midpoint notch. Stitch to the notch (see step **3** on p. 123). Fold the top right sides together to align the remaining midpoint notch with the center mark. Stitch from the notch to the center in the same manner (see step **4** on p. 123).

Use a border (see the illustration on p. 106 and the sidebar on p. 107) or your choice of embellishment on the crown piece. When pinning a border in place, check to make sure the border matches at the center back before stitching. Stitch using a large zigzag. If necessary, stitch down the folds of the miters if they puff out.

Bind the lower edge of the crown piece with spandex binding (see step **5** on p. 122). Gently stretch the binding and fleece while stitching. Place the center-back edges of the crown right sides together and stitch using a long straight stitch with ⅜-in. seam allowance. Backstitch to secure the end of the stitching line at the bound edge (see step **6** on p. 122).

Cut three pieces of fleece in coordinating colors (or the same color) into ⅜-in. crosswise grain strips the full width of the fabric. Stretch the strips firmly. Cut three 6-in.-long pieces from each strip. Twist three strips together (one from each color fleece) at the center and fold them in half. Make three tassels in this manner. Braid the remaining strips into two 10-in. to 12-in. lengths, finishing them with a slip knot

at the ends. Trim the excess to 2 in. below the knot. (See the sidebar on p. 125 for more information on fleece cording.)

Place the crown and the top right sides together, matching the points on the top and crown. Match midpoint notches from the top to the bottom of the V's on the crown. Pin in place. With the top on the bed of the machine, stitch, starting at the center back and using a ⅜-in. seam allowance. Pivot with the needle dropped at the inside corners. A few stitch lengths before the point, drop the needle. Raise the presser foot and insert a tassel between the layers so that only ⅛ in. at the base of the tassel extends from the point. Stitch back and forth across the end of the point several times to secure in place. Drop the needle, pivot, and turn to continue stitching the other side of the point, being careful not to catch the tassel in the stitching (see step **7** on p. 123).

When stitching the tassels in place, set the needle position to the far left for stitching around the bulk at the narrow part of the point. Clip into the V on the crown and trim excess fleece at the points. Do not trim the twist

in the tassel from the wrong side because it makes the tassel easier to pull out.

Pin one end of the premade braid to the wrong side of the binding at the base of the earflap. Use a bar tack to secure the braid in place on the right side. Trim the knot and any excess above the bar tack so the wrong side is smooth and flat.

To attach the bells, cut one end of the tassel strip to a point, twist it in your fingers to compress it, and thread it through the top of a bell. Tie the tassel in a square knot with another tassel strip. Secure the bell more permanently by hand-stitching through the knot or by squeezing some fabric glue on the center of the knot.

To make this hat in adult sizes, slash the crown pattern vertically through the points, spread the pattern, and add width evenly (divided three ways) at these points until the crown measures the desired head size (see the illustration on p. 124). Redraw the lower edge, adding ½ in. to 1 in. in length. Add height to the crown by slashing it across the crown and spreading the pattern. Slash the top piece through the points to the center mark and spread

MAKING THE TRIPOINT HAT

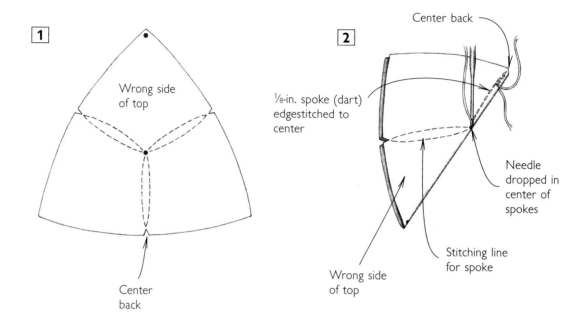

1

Wrong side
of top

Center
back

2

Center back

⅛-in. spoke (dart)
edgestitched to
center

Needle
dropped in
center of
spokes

Stitching line
for spoke

Wrong side
of top

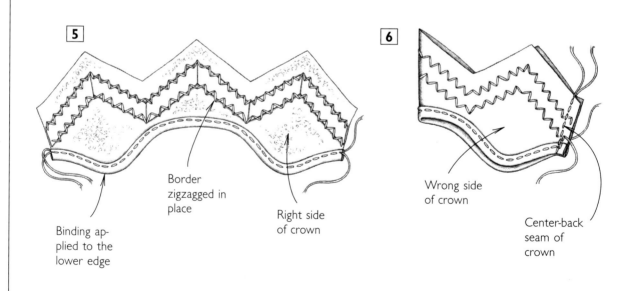

5

Border
zigzagged in
place

Right side
of crown

Binding ap-
plied to the
lower edge

6

Wrong side
of crown

Center-back
seam of
crown

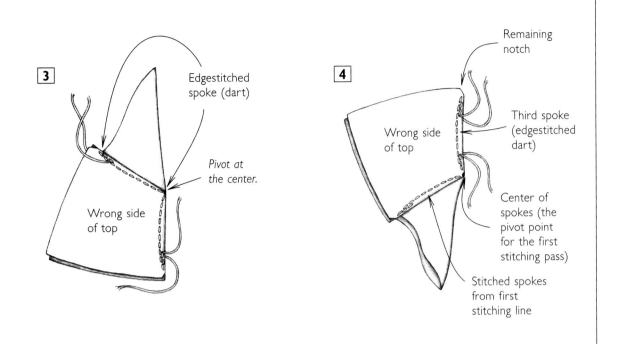

3 Edgestitched spoke (dart)

Pivot at the center.

Wrong side of top

4 Remaining notch

Wrong side of top

Third spoke (edgestitched dart)

Center of spokes (the pivot point for the first stitching pass)

Stitched spokes from first stitching line

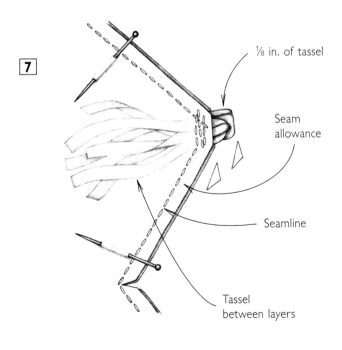

7 ⅛ in. of tassel

Seam allowance

Seamline

Tassel between layers

Crown pattern

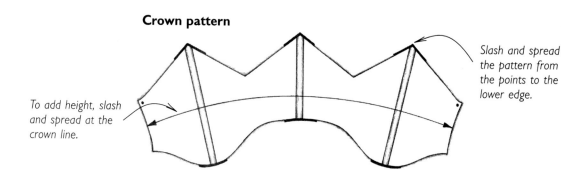

To add height, slash
and spread at the
crown line.

*Slash and spread
the pattern from
the points to the
lower edge.*

*To make adult sizes in the Tripoint
hat, slash through the crown pattern
from the points to the lower edge.
Spread evenly at each slash until the
pattern measures the desired crown
measurement (above). Slash the top
pattern and add the same amount as
was added to the crown at the points
(right). Redraw the outer edges of
the pattern to create the new cutting
line for the larger pattern. (To create
a pattern for baby sizes, reverse the
process by overlapping pattern
pieces.)*

Top pattern

*Slash and spread
the pattern from
the points to the
center.*

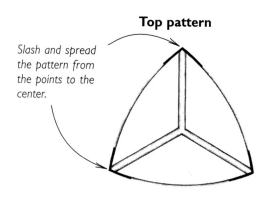

the pattern the same amount that was added to the crown points. Extend the cutting lines from the existing lines on both pattern pieces to create new points. To make the pattern smaller for infants and babies, reverse the process by overlapping the pattern pieces.

HEADBAND

A headband like the one in the top illustration on p. 126 can be an excellent ear-warmer. It is perfect for sunny-but-cold autumn days when the wind gives you an ice-cream headache but you aren't ready to commit to hat season. Hook-and-loop tape makes on and off and size

Design Details with Fleece Cording

Cording made from fleece makes a very nice edge finish that is especially effective for finishing irregular edges (see the border edges on Maddie's vest on p. 32). It can be used to outline appliqués, to make braids (this cording works especially well as soutache braids), and to make curly tassels (see the Tripoint hat on p. 119). It can also be used as a thick thread for stitching (see Decorative stitches on p. 65).

To make the cording, cut strips of fleece in the crossgrain. The fabric will curl to the wrong side when pulled firmly. Remember that you are trying to pull it out of shape, so don't be afraid to really yank on it (see the photo below). If the cord breaks, it probably means that it should be cut slightly wider. Experiment with different widths for different uses. I've found that somewhere between ¼ in. and ½ in. usually works best, but the cording should be narrower for soutache and wider for edge finishes.

Larger cording can be made by cutting the strip a little wider. Pull the strip to create the curled edge and hand-stitch in place. Catch both cut edges when whip-stitching the large cording to the garment. The results of this method can be seen on Sarah's coat (p. 43) at the lower edge of the overlay.

To use the cording like a soutache braid, draw the design on the main fabric with a wash-out marker. Cut the cording, stretch it, then zigzag or straight-stitch the cording in place. A special cording foot on your sewing machine may be helpful in this process.

Pocket openings and button-holes can be cut out of the main fabric and then edge-finished with cording as seen on p. 90.

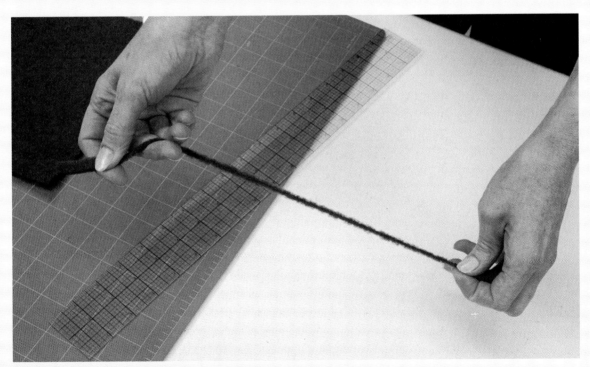

Pull hard on the fleece strip to make cording. If it breaks, cut the next strip a little wider.

adjustments easy. And fleece with a wind barrier, two bonded layers, or a double layer at the ear area adds extra protection.

This headband requires:

- ⅛ yd. of fleece or pile, any weight
- 60 in. of 1½-in.-wide nylon/spandex binding
- 2-in. strip of ¾-in.-wide loop tape
- 1-in. strip of ¾-in.-wide hook tape

Transfer the pattern to a 1-in. grid (see the pattern below). Bind the top and bottom edges of the fleece without stretching using nylon/spandex (see Binding on p. 65). Fold the ends of the

HEADBAND WITH DOUBLE LAYER AT THE EARS

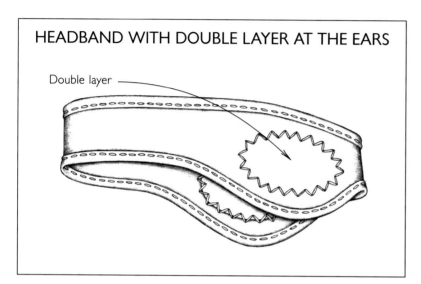

Double layer

HEADBAND PATTERN

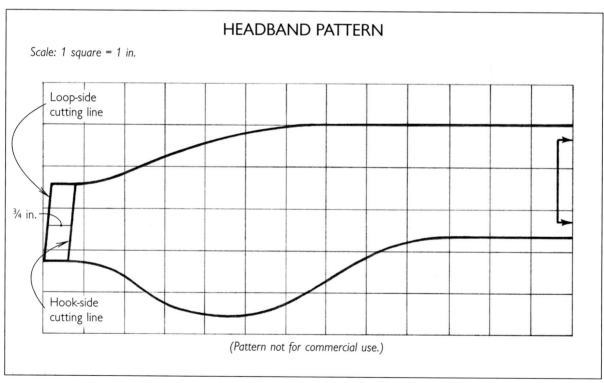

Scale: 1 square = 1 in.

Loop-side cutting line

¾ in.

Hook-side cutting line

(Pattern not for commercial use.)

HOOK-AND-LOOP CLOSURE ON A HEADBAND

Stitch the loop tape to the wrong side of the headband and the hook tape to the right side.

Wrong side
of headband

Stretch
binding

2-in. strip
of loop tape
stitched in
place

Ends folded
under and
stitched

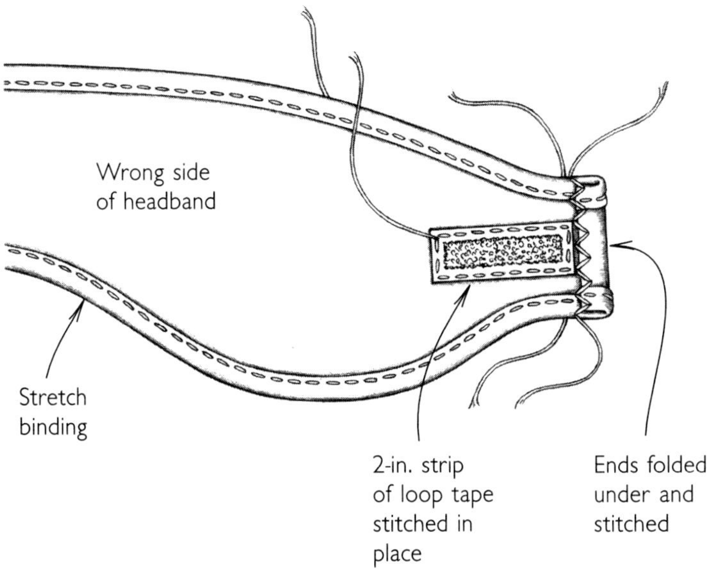

headband under ⅜ in. and stitch in place. Apply a 2-in. strip of ¾-in.-wide loop tape to the wrong side of the longer end of the headband and a 1-in. strip of ¾-in.-wide hook tape to the right side of the shorter end of the headband (see the illustration above). For extra protection at the ears, cut a small, ear-sized patch of fleece and zigzag it to the inside of the headband at the ear area (see the top illustration on the facing page).

MITTENS AND GLOVES

As we mentioned earlier, pattern companies, as well as some fabric stores, are providing a variety of accessory patterns that include mittens (see Resources on p. 131). Some options for the mitten patterns may be: an outer shell of waterproof/water-repellent fabrics, longer cuffs, or an opposable thumb more conducive to snow sports.

Here are some tips to keep in mind for mittens:

• Use a narrow seam allow-ance, or stitch with a wider seam allowance and trim after stitching.

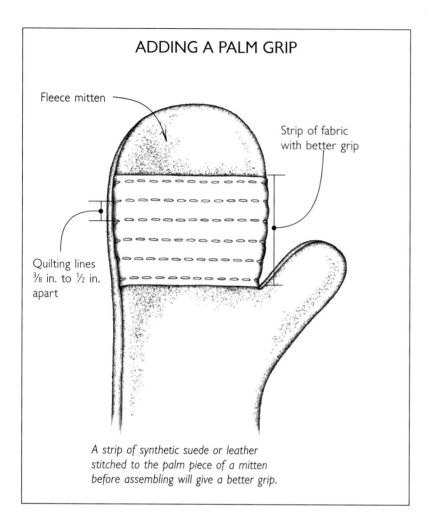

ADDING A PALM GRIP

Fleece mitten

Strip of fabric with better grip

Quilting lines ⅜ in. to ½ in. apart

A strip of synthetic suede or leather stitched to the palm piece of a mitten before assembling will give a better grip.

- Double-stitch deep corners, like where the thumb connects to the hand. These areas get a lot of stress and can pull out easily.
- Clip the seam allowance all the way to the stitching line at the corners.
- For better gripping capability, stitch a strip of another fabric across the palm piece before assembling. Use synthetic leather or suede, or investigate your own possibilities in your fabric stash. Stitch some quilting lines across the strip at ⅜-in. to ½-in. intervals so that the strip doesn't buckle (see the illustration at left).
- A water-repellent woven nylon can be machine-quilted to the top of the mitten before assembly to give extra wind protection without making the mitten too warm.
- If possible, use a flatlock seam for the outside edge seam. It gives a flatter, smoother inside edge and is easier to finish because you don't have to turn it. (You won't be able to topstitch through the seam as is recommended on p. 56 because of how tight the curve is on the pattern piece.)

Glove patterns are also available but require intricate manipulating during the construction process. I don't recommend them for a beginning sewer, but a moderate- to experienced-level sewer can try a lightweight stretch fleece (Polartec 100S) for a great pair of gloves.

SCARVES

Another accessory in the no-sew category is a scarf, or muffler. For the sewing process, refer to the blanket-stitch instructions on p. 65, as well as the blanket instructions at the beginning of this chapter (pp. 102-109). The only differences between the scarf and the blanket are the size and possibly the edge. Other edge finishes we've shown—borders, bindings, embroidered trims—will all finish a scarf nicely.

Preshaped scarves with a cowl feature or some other sewn-in shape are available as patterns and would be a nice addition to a variety of cold-weather styles. Or try a new slant on a scarf or hood with a "snood." Available

through major pattern companies, this is a terrific option for a dressier look. This combination hood and scarf has a loop at the neck for pulling the other end through. It's warm and sophisticated with a lot of options for embellishing. Try it with two layers of 100-weight fabric in two colors stitched and topstitched or bound together.

Other areas to consider for your own fleece research and development include costumes, stuffed toys, car-seat covers, coats for pets, horse blankets or warmers, and diaper wraps with a vapor barrier. With new developments each year in fleece and pile, thinner profiles, and more fashion-oriented styles, the options seem infinite. It's almost scary to think that this is just the beginning of an era of new, more comfortable synthetics—and that's from a dyed-in-the-wool, natural-fiber lover!

Resources

U.S. Resources

The Bee Lee Co.
PO Box 36108
Dallas, TX 75235-1108
(800) 527-5271
Snaps, zippers, thread, catalog

Birch Street Clothing Inc.
1021 S. Claremont Street
San Mateo, CA 94402
(800) 736-0854
(415) 570-4292 (fax)
birchst@ix.netcom.com
Prym snaps and attacher,
catalog

C.O.D. Fabric Outlet
12675 S.W. Broadway
Beaverton, OR 97005
(503) 641-7271
Fabrics, patterns, notions,
swatches

Denver Fabrics
2777 W. Belleview
Littleton, CO 80123
(800) 996-6902
(303) 730-2778 (fax)
df@denverfabrics.com
http:\\www.denverfabrics.com
Fabrics, patterns, notions,
swatches, personal shopper

Famous Labels
2107 N.E. Burnside Rd.
Gresham, OR 97030
(503) 666-3187
Fabrics, notions, swatches

Frostline Kits
2525 River Rd.
Grand Junction, CO 81505
(800) KITS-USA
http:\\www.frostlinekits.com
Fabrics, patterns, notions,
kits, swatches, catalog

G Street Fabrics Mail Order
12240 Wilkins Ave.
Rockville, MD 20852
(800) 333-9191
(301) 231-9155 (fax)
Fabrics, patterns, notions,
swatches, flyer

The Green Pepper
1285 River Rd.
Eugene, OR 97404
(541) 689-3292
(541) 689-3591 (fax)
Fabrics, patterns, notions,
swatches, hardware, catalog,
wholesale available

Hot Tools Division
PO Box 615
Marblehead, MA 01945
(617) 639-1000
Hot tools, tips, catalog

Joyce's Fabrics

PO Box 381 RH
Morrisville, NY 13408-0381
Fabrics, patterns, zippers,
snaps, swatches ($2 with
SASE), mail order only

Malden Mills Outlet Store

2401 Utah Ave., Suite 150
Seattle, WA 98134
(206) 682-7037
(206) 682-7061 (fax)
Fabrics (color cards—10-yd.
minimum), wholesale available

Mt. Mend

6655 Arapaho Ave., Suite B
Boulder, CO 80303
(303) 443-1925
Notions, snaps, zippers,
equipment repair

Oregon Tailor Supply

2123-A S.E. Division
Portland, OR 97202
(503) 232-6191
Notions, snaps, zippers

Outdoor Wilderness Fabrics

16415 N. Midland Blvd.
Nampa, ID 83651
(800) 693-7467 (phone orders)
(208) 466-1602 (information)
(800) 333-6930 (fax)
Fabrics, patterns, notions,
swatches, catalog, wholesale
available

Quest Outfitters

619 Cattlemen Rd.
Sarasota, FL 34232
(800) 359-6931
(941) 377-5105 (fax)
Fabrics, patterns, notions,
swatches, catalog

Ragged Mountain Equipment

PO Box 130
Intervale, NH 03845
(603) 356-3042
Fabrics, patterns, notions,
zippers

The Rain Shed

707 N.W. 11th
Corvallis, OR 97330
(541) 753-8900
(541) 757-1887 (fax)
Fabrics, patterns, notions,
swatches, catalog

RCT Fabrics

2801 N.W. Nela
Portland, OR 97210
(800) 482-4990 (retail)
(800) RCT-5666 (for samples)
http:\\www.rctfabrics.com
Fabrics, swatches, inventory
list on web site

Seattle Fabrics

8702 Aurora Ave. N.
Seattle, WA 98103
(206) 525-0670
(206) 525-0779 (fax)
Fabrics, patterns, notions,
swatches, catalog

The Sewing Workshop
2010 Balboa
San Francisco, CA 94121
(800) 466-1599
Patterns

Wy'East Fabrics
PO Box 7328
2895 Valpak Rd.
Salem, OR 97303
(503) 364-8419
(503) 391-8057 (fax)
sales@wyeastfabrics.com
http://www.wyeastfabrics.
com/~tarpsusa
Fabrics, patterns, notions,
swatches, equipment repair,
catalog

Canadian Resources

Evelyn's Sewing Centre
17817 Leslie St., Unit 40
Newmarket, Ont., Canada
L3Y 8C6
(905) 853-7001
Fabrics, patterns, notions

Jalie Patterns
2478 Martel
Saint Romuald, Que., Canada
G6W 6L2
(418) 839-7214
(418) 839-9599 (fax)
Over 100 outerwear patterns

MacPhee Workshop
Box 10, Site 16
R.R. 8
Edmonton, Alta., Canada
T5L 4H8
1-888-MAC-PHEE (toll free)
(403) 973-3516
(403) 973-6216 (fax)
hmacphee@macpheeworkshop.
com
http://www.macpheeworkshop.
com
Fabrics, patterns, notions,
catalog

Sundrop Outerwear Textiles
140-1140 Austin Ave.
Coquitlam, B.C., Canada
V3K 3P5
(604) 936-5236
Outerwear and activewear
fabrics, patterns, notions,
catalog

Textile Outfitters
735 10th Ave. SW
Calgary, Alta., Canada
T2R 0B3
(403) 543-7676
(403) 543-7677 (fax)
Outerwear and activewear
fabrics, catalog

Index

Index

135

BOOK PUBLISHER: Jim Childs

ACQUISITIONS EDITOR: Jolynn Gower

PUBLISHING COORDINATOR: Sarah Coe

EDITOR: Jennifer Renjilian

DESIGNER & LAYOUT ARTIST: Amy L. Bernard

PHOTOGRAPHER, EXCEPT WHERE NOTED: Jack Deutsch

ILLUSTRATOR: Christine Erikson

TYPEFACES: Caxton, Giltus

PAPER: 70-lb. Moistrite Matte

PRINTER: Quebecor Printing/Hawkins,
         Church Hill, Tennessee